JUGGLING

JUGGLING

Learn all the techniques of juggling from the basics to the most complex

STUART ASHMAN

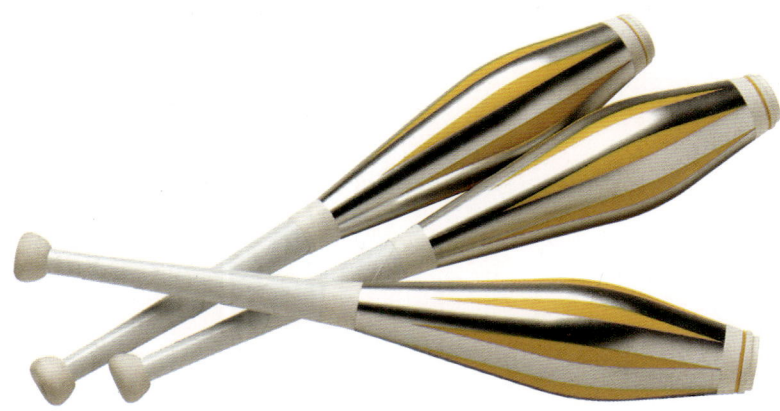

Bath • New York • Singapore • Hong Kong • Cologne • Delhi
Melbourne • Amsterdam • Johannesburg • Auckland • Shenzhen

This edition published in 2012

Parragon
Queen Street House
4 Queen Street
Bath BA1 1HE, UK

www.parragon.com

Copyright © Parragon Book Ltd 2000

Designed, packaged and produced by
Stonecastle Graphics Ltd

Photography by Pinpoint
Edited by Philip de Ste. Croix
Models: Lisa Ashman, Stuart Ashman, Richard Dwyer

All rights reserved. No part of this publication may be reproduced, stored in a retrieval system, or transmitted in any way or by any means, electronic, mechanical, photocopying, recording or otherwise, without
the prior permission of the copyright holder.

ISBN 978-1-4454-7537-0

Manufactured in China

Contents

Introduction 6

THE BASICS
Getting Started 8
The Stance and the Jugglespace 10

STAGE 1
LEARNING THE CASCADE
One Ball 12
Two Balls 14
Three Balls 16
Why Cant I...? 18

STAGE 2
THE WORLD OF THE THREE BALLS
Now We're Started... 22
The High Throw 24
The First Tricks 26
Over the Top 28
Under the Leg 30
Behind the Back 32
Two Balls in One Hand 34
Tricks with Two in One Hand 36

STAGE 3
GETTING FANCY
The Snatch 38
The Chop 40
The Shower 42
Two Classic Three-Ball Tricks 44
Having a Three-Ball Ball 46
The Neck Catch 48
Using the Body 50

STAGE 4
THERE'S MORE TO LIFE THAN THREE BALLS
Crazy for Numbers 52
Juggling with Clubs 54
Juggling with Rings 58
How to Juggle with Anything 60
Put the Book Down! 62
Further Reading 64

INTRODUCTION

JUGGLING IS no five-minute fad soon forgotten. Juggling is pictured in ancient Egyptian friezes dating from 2000 BCE; it was among the entertainments at the great medieval fairs and part of the performances of magicians and mountebanks long before that. More recently, jugglers have held down top billing in variety theaters and music halls; many went on to be comic stars of the silver screen; now they have reappeared in the street circuses, cabarets, and spectacles of the 21st century.

Nowadays, you might see jugglers anywhere – a beach, a park, or a street corner. Juggling is no longer a closely guarded secret passed down in circus families or from teacher to apprentice. That's just not the way we do things any more; today, it's easy to learn from other jugglers and you are encouraged to do so. This book is part of that process.

Juggling is also, I have to point out, extremely good for your coordination and left brain/right brain balance. But better still, it's fun—fun you can have on your own and fun you can share with others. People can be as amazed by your skills as were the audiences in ancient Egypt and the bazaars of Baghdad. With other jugglers you can swap tricks and work out even more complex ways to juggle.

There's more not in this book than there is in it, but I'm starting to juggle with words and you've just been given three balls to do that with. So let's get going!

INTRODUCTION

THE BASICS

Getting Started

WELCOME TO your juggling book. It's not a book that juggles; it's a book that will help *you* to juggle. It's not really a book to juggle with, but by the end you'll be able to do even that...if it takes your fancy.

Juggling is easy to learn. I've known people to pick it up in half an hour—but most take a little longer, so don't worry if you are not as quick as that. Practice is very important; you've got to teach yourself new habits, just as when you learn to ride a bike, and repetition is the only effective way to do this. The book is designed to introduce you to a new skill on every double-page spread (with a few exceptions, which you'll discover along the way). When you are working through the first part and most of the second, it is important that you can do the sequence described on one page before moving on to the next, because the skills build on one another.

THE BASICS

Patience!

The book comes with a set of balls that are ideal to learn with—but you can juggle virtually anything, any kind of ball from Ping-Pong to cannon! Someone is bound to ask you to demonstrate with tennis balls, but you'd better wait until you have mastered the basics before trying that. Tennis balls are very light and bouncy and tend to hop straight out of your hand before you can catch them.

That is not a good way to start. This is.

The Stance and the Jugglespace

THE WAY we stand or sit when attempting any skillful task will affect our performance. Correct posture, if learned and applied at this stage, will help prevent problems developing in the future.

1. Be comfortable. Your feet should be slightly apart, legs relaxed and bent at the knees.
2. Your hands should be at waist level, palms up and held at the side of your body.
3. Shoulders relaxed.
4. Eyes looking straight ahead at a point just above forehead height.

It might help if I introduce an important, imaginary concept at this point.

Imagine that in front of you is a sheet of glass, or an invisible frame like those used for windows or pictures. The bottom corners are your two hands, the top is in a line just above head height (see photograph left). For the basic juggling pattern all the balls must remain within that plane, the sheet of glass, or the frame (right). I call it **"the jugglespace"** for short. There is no agreement on the use of that word among jugglers in general, but I like it.

THE BASICS

STAGE 1
LEARNING THE CASCADE

One Ball

PLACE ONE ball in your stronger hand (the one you normally use for writing or holding tools) with your palm face up, and throw it to the other hand (right). Yes I know it's easy—but take time to watch the arc that the ball makes as it travels through the imaginary plane of the sheet of glass that I told you about on the previous page.

Important Rule No.1: Juggling is about accurate throwing, not just catching.

Try to make your throw with one ball so accurate—the arc of its flight peaking just above head

LEARNING THE CASCADE

height—that you don't have to move your other hand to catch it. All throws and catches at this stage should be made palm up and done at waist height (above).

Now repeat this throw with the other hand. If this is your weaker hand, really concentrate on the accuracy of the arc; your catching hand should not have to move much to catch the ball.

Yeah, I know this stuff seems so dull...but it's the groundwork to stop you getting stuck on the problem pages later on. Trust me and give it some time.

Two Balls

TAKE A ball in each hand, palms facing up, feeling relaxed, deep breaths—now, as before, throw a ball from one hand to the other. Just as it peaks in that arc you have learned (below), throw the second ball to the other hand (below right). *Wait* before you try this.

Important Rule No.2: The second ball should be thrown up and over to the other hand.

Some of you—and you know who you are—will try to pass the second ball directly to the other

LEARNING THE CASCADE

hand without throwing it upward. At this stage always throw *up*, whichever hand you are using.

1. Keep the arcs consistent. Different heights will make one hand rush to catch the ball.
2. Stop after the two throws. Keeping the motion going is a hard trick to be learned later.
3. Count out loud as the throws reach the peak of the arcs:

"One...Two..." It sounds stupid but somehow the brain tells the hands, when it is the right time to throw!

Stay practicing this stage until your throws are really good; do not turn the page—work, work, work—trust me!

By the time you can work with two balls properly, you are over halfway to juggling and already past the hard stage.

Three Balls

IF YOU *can't* throw two balls with confidence with accurate throws—and no drops—then turn back a page and practice, practice...and practice some more. If you can do it, glad to have you still with us...

Take the third ball, hold it in your strong hand—you now have two balls in that hand (below).

Important rule No.3: Don't panic!

That's all: remember your stance, the jugglespace, and the imaginary sheet of glass.

1. The ball farthest away from you in the hand holding the two balls throws first.
2. As the first ball peaks (below), throw the second ball from the other hand—as in the two-ball stuff.

LEARNING THE CASCADE

Confused? Just think that each throw is clearing a hand to catch the next ball! Confident? Now try to put an extra throw in. The fourth throw will bring two balls back to the start hand. Why stop now? Keep the pattern going, counting your throws to beat your record. You may find you get stuck on one total for a while—we all do—but after 30 throws you can say you are really juggling—because you must have made a few mistakes and corrected them! Time to learn some tricks!

3. When ball number two peaks (top of page), throw the third ball across (above), and catch it in the hand that holds ball one. If you have caught all three—congratulations! You are now juggling!

Why Can't I...?

ON THIS spread we'll look at some common juggling problems. Strange but true: not everybody juggles on their first attempt! However, if you have spent at least half an hour trying to get to the third ball, then there are only a few reasons why you are not juggling.

1. I don't have time to throw the third ball.

Sometimes you may find that the second ball is caught in the hand that is still holding the third ball. It has been a lot to take in, so at this stage the brain needs some help to sort things out!

Solution: Counting out loud as the ball peaks on each throw will send a message to your hand and help you to release the ball at the correct time. I don't know why but this does work—but the counting must be done *out loud*.

2. I can't help passing the second ball to my other hand instead of throwing it up (below)!

Even though you have spent time on the two-ball exercise, when

LEARNING THE CASCADE

confronted with three balls, what I call the old "schoolyard" throw starts to return.

Solution: Swap the two balls (in the first-throw hand) over to your other hand. You are probably starting with your strong hand, but the weaker hand is usually more open and amenable to learning a new skill!

3. I only drop some throws, not all of them.

You can be tempted to try to catch a throw too early, either by snatching it (catching with the palm down) or trying to take the ball too high (below left and right).

Solution: Wait until the ball is about waist height and catch it palm up.

Why Can't I...?

MORE ANSWERS from the juggling doctor's clinic.

4. I have to move across the room to maintain any sort of juggle (below)!

It can be good exercise but "sprint juggling," as it is called, is very frustrating for the beginner.
Solution: Remember the analogy of the sheet of glass (see pages 10–11). Throwing a ball either forward or behind the correct plane will result in the next throw being even worse. As throws tend to be away from the body, your only option is to reach forward, and it's a downward spiral from there. Go back to practicing with two balls and really concentrate on accurate throws. Standing in front of a wall can cure sprint juggling; it hurts!

5. The balls collide in the air and I'm left with empty hands.

The heart starts to pump and the hands sweat, when you have three balls to juggle for the first time—throwing too fast can be the brain's way of trying to cope with the problem.
Solution As in problem 1, take a deep breath and count out loud as the balls peak, to help you establish a comfortable, unhurried juggling rhythm.

LEARNING THE CASCADE

6. I simply can't grasp the three-ball, throwing sequence in my head!

Solution: Throw all the balls in the correct order (right) but don't bother to catch them (below). The correct juggling pattern will leave two balls together on the floor on your left (if you started with your right hand) and one on the floor on the right (if you started with your left) (below right).

JUGGLING

Stage 2

THE WORLD OF THE THREE BALLS

Now We're Started...

WHAT YOU have just learned is called "the cascade" in technical, juggler talk. It is the basis of everything that follows.

From now on, although some of the skills in the later pages build upon routines I explain first, there is nothing to stop you trying out two or three different things at once. In fact, it's a lot more fun that way. Try and be ahead of yourself, especially when practicing a skill that you've nearly "got": vary your practice by putting other moves in, and soon you'll find you are building up sequences of tricks that naturally go together.

Always keep your juggling balls somewhere that you can find them when the fancy takes you—four minutes of spontaneous fun is often better than half an hour of set practice. Juggling with music playing is great, too—sequences of moves seem to flow out of the rhythms.

THE WORLD OF THE THREE BALLS

HOT TIP
I have already mentioned counting out loud. Count each ball as it reaches the top of its arc. Even if it sounds daft, it <u>really helps</u> your practice, your rhythm, and your concentration.

One last thing. It's always important to master everything you do *with both hands*. That way you can do many more impressive tricks, and make the most out of each new skill. Of course, one hand is likely to be better than the other—in this book we refer to them as the strong and weak hands to avoid confusion. To hop back to our jugglespace for a moment: imagine that it is divided in half, vertically down the middle—the central axis of your body (bottom right). Everything that you do on one side of the dividing line should be mirrored on the other.

The High Throw

WHILE JUGGLING three balls, it's good practice to try and speed up or slow down the pattern. This is done by altering the height of the throws. Consistently high throws with all three balls will give a slow pattern; low throws will make you juggle faster.

Got that? Perhaps you're ready for your first trick. When trying any new trick, it's good to break it down into easy stages.

1. Throw one ball high into the air (right) and practice catching it with either hand.
2. Now hold a ball in the catching hand, releasing it just before you catch the high throw, and throwing it in the normal way to the other hand.
3. Repeat step 2, this time with your other hand.
4. Now try the trick while juggling normally.

THE WORLD OF THE THREE BALLS

HOT TIP
While the high throw is in the air, hold on to the other two balls for a moment— a beat or two is missed in the rhythm of the pattern. The high ball and the delay before the next throw give you time to do more difficult tricks, which we'll come to later.

The First Tricks

WHEN YOU send the high throw into the air—whether it's just a short distance higher than your normal pattern in the jugglespace or if it goes as high as you can possibly throw it while still holding some hope of catching it again—you have suddenly given yourself time. Time in which you can do something else; something that nobody expects. This is the beginning of making *tricks* that can surprise and delight yourself, or an audience, or anyone to whom you're showing off.

So what can you do with that short spare moment? Here are some suggestions. I am sure you can come up with excellent ones of your own.

1. Swap the other two balls over.
2. Bang the two balls together (right), or clap (more difficult).
3. Pirouette—turn right round really fast.
4. Somersault (if you are gymnastic).
5. Sing a little song (whether you are musical or not).
6. Pinch someone's hat, drink, or ice-cream cone (if you're cheeky).

THE WORLD OF THE THREE BALLS

Over the Top

NOW FOR your first real trick. Until now, all throws have been made underneath the arc of the descending ball, inside the pattern. Now try throwing *outside* the pattern to the other hand: the ball seems to fly over the top of the juggle.

As with most juggling tricks, it is easier to break this down into a sequence, using two balls, and then extend it to three.

1. With a ball in each hand, throw a normal arc with your weak hand; as the ball peaks, throw an outside throw with the strong hand (pictures right). The second throw will take longer to reach the other hand.
2. Now try it with three balls (page 29). It may seem strange to make the adjustment for the outside arc; more time spent practicing at stage 1 will make this seem easier after a while.

THE WORLD OF THE THREE BALLS

Any new trick should be practiced with both hands—try to master it with your weak hand as well as with your dominant hand. The same trick performed with both hands produces a *reverse-cascade* juggling pattern—and that's very impressive. Or try returning the over the top throw immediately to the original hand with a mirror throw. If you can keep this going, especially with a different colored ball, it looks great—the ball seems to go backward and forward over the other two, like a game of tennis.

Under the Leg

ALL THROUGH the book so far, I have emphasized the image of the "sheet of glass" (see pages 10–11) and how important it is to juggle consistently in one plane. Now it's time to forget it! After a while you will want to attempt the *under-the-leg trick*—oh yes, you will! Here's how you do it.

1. Take just one ball in your strong hand, throw it under your nearer leg, and over to the other hand. You may find it easier to bend your leg slightly and throw under the knee (right).
2. Now with two balls repeat stage 1, but the second throw is a normal cascade throw to the other hand, which is now back in front. Catch it!
3. Try throwing the normal arc first—then the under-the-leg throw (top left, page 31).
4. Now juggle with three balls. The throw before the trick with your weak hand should be pitched slightly higher. This gives you valuable extra time to bring your hand down and under your leg (far right)—releasing the ball on the other side with an accurate hop to the other hand—and then back to the front again.

THE WORLD OF THE THREE BALLS

HOT TIP

Remember to count out loud: "one" when the first higher throw peaks, "two" when throwing under the leg, and "three" when you revert to the cascade.

As always, try with the other leg, then practice with both—right/left, right/left. Also attempt throws under the leg on the other side from the trick throw—i.e. under the left leg with the right hand, and vice versa.

Behind the Back

THIS TRICK uses virtually the same principles that you have just learned for the *under-the-leg* throw.

1. Take a ball in your strong hand and pass it in a smooth arc behind your back, releasing the ball level with the base of your opposite shoulder blade (i.e. if you are throwing right-handed, the ball should be released behind your left shoulder blade). The ball should continue to travel up and appear to hop over your shoulder (below left) and down into the waiting palm of the other hand.

THE WORLD OF THE THREE BALLS

2. With two balls, one in each hand, wait for the trick throw to peak over your shoulder (bottom right, page 32), before releasing the second ball from your weak hand in a normal throw to your dominant hand.
3. As a variation, try throwing the trick throw as the second throw of a sequence.

As always, try to master the trick with both hands, then you will be able to do continuous throws with both hands! Juggling without being able to see your hands (below): pretty impressive!

> **HOT TIP**
> The shoulder over which you are going to throw the trick throw should be relaxed and dropped slightly for best results.

Two Balls in One Hand

ONE POSSIBLE definition of juggling is *the manipulation of more balls than you are using hands*, so two balls in one hand is definitely juggling

1. In your stronger hand, hold two balls. As in the *three-ball cascade*, the ball farthest away from you is the first to be thrown in this pattern.

2. Release the ball vertically upward, throwing it away from the central axis of your body, and slightly higher than you would in your normal cascade arc. As it peaks, throw the second ball in the same path as the first (below left).

3. Your hand should then move over to catch the first ball (below), and then the second.

THE WORLD OF THE THREE BALLS

HOT TIP
The imaginary sheet of glass has made a welcome return—the balls will move in a circle in this plane (clockwise using the right hand, counterclockwise with the left)—you will find out why later! Your hand just makes sideways movements, catching and throwing. Now try the same pattern with your weak hand.

Another way of juggling two balls in one hand is by *throwing in columns*. The balls rise up vertically, falling back down again in the same path or column (right). Time the second throw to happen when the first ball peaks; the throwing hand just makes sideways movements to allow space for the balls to rise and fall.

Tricks with Two in One Hand

WITH YOUR strong hand juggling *two in one*, as we have just learned, the other hand can simply throw the third ball vertically in time with one of the other balls, or you can "cheat" the trick by just moving your hand up and down with the ball still in it!

For best results show the third ball with your hand upright and the palm facing away from you toward the audience. Be ambidextrous! If you're solid on doing columns with one hand, then try the same tricks with them, too.

One up, Two up

1. While juggling three balls, throw one up the middle of the cascade (below), as in the high throw.
2. When the ball peaks, the remaining two balls in either hand should be thrown

THE WORLD OF THE THREE BALLS

simultaneously in vertical column throws (below), which will eventually land back to the same hands.

3. As in the high throw, you can decide which hand will catch the descending center ball. Sometimes it's effective to alternate the hands that make the catch.

The Yo-Yo

While juggling columns, hold a ball with your other hand over the ball that you are throwing nearest to the central axis of your body (above). Move this hand up and down in time with the ball, thereby giving the impression that the balls are attached by an invisible string. A similar trick features an imaginary magnet.

Stage 3
GETTING FANCY

The Snatch

WE'VE JUST experimented with the way you throw. Now try changing the way you catch.

1. Throw a ball from your weak hand, to your strong hand but catch it with your palm down (below and right)—snatch it!
2. Now throw the ball back, releasing it with the palm up.
3. Place a ball in each hand, throw the normal two-ball cascade pattern, but snatch the ball with your strong hand, taking it at the peak of the arc.

GETTING FANCY

4. Juggle normally with three balls, and cue the trick on a throw from your weak hand, snatching the ball as it peaks (above left and right), and put it back into the cascade.

HOT TIP
The arc of the snatched ball should be higher than the normal cascade, the catch—if taken at the peak of the trajectory—will give you more time to bring the ball down, turn your hand round, and execute a normal throw.

Try it with the other hand—be ambidextrous! Then you can attempt to snatch every throw with both hands; you will need to transfer the ball with a palm-down action—a flick—which will put a spin on the ball. Remember to pitch each throw higher than the normal cascade pattern.

WARNING
This trick will seriously impress everybody!

The Chop

FOR CHOPS we go straight into using two balls, one in each hand. Why? Because you deserve it!

1. With your strong hand raised to its highest point in the plane of the sheet of glass, throw the other ball in a normal arc, **but**, as it ascends, bring your arm down toward the central axis of your body (below left), so the moving ball travels under the arm (below). This movement can be done quite slowly at first.

2. When your strong hand reaches the lower level of the "sheet of glass," it releases its ball with a little hop toward the other hand (right).

GETTING FANCY

3. The strong hand then quickly returns to catch the descending first ball, which is still in its normal arc (above right).
4. Now while juggling with three balls, pitch a throw slightly higher with your weak hand, catch the ball at the top of the arc with your strong hand, bring it down—arm straight—Ω and into the center of the pattern with the next throw traveling underneath as you have just learned.

HOT TIP
The next throw with your weak hand should be higher than normal, to give some time for the little hop after the chop, and to catch the higher ball.

With practice the downward movement of the straight arm will become faster, like a karate chop through the air. Be ambidextrous, and continuous—now you're getting seriously hot!

The Shower

CAST YOUR mind back to learning *the cascade* with two balls. We said you must only throw the ball *up*, not pass it from one hand to the other by the short route. This time, that's exactly what you have to do. If you were doing this before, it wasn't wrong, you just weren't ready for it...Now you are!

1. Take two balls, one in each hand, and do that schoolyard thing. Toss a ball into the air as an *over-the-top* throw with your strong hand, and pass the other ball by the short route to the strong hand. Actually, it's more of a slap of the ball from one hand to the other.

GETTING FANCY

2. Now for three balls. Take two in your strong hand and just go for it (page 42). As soon as you have thrown the first ball, send the second up, following the same path as the first, and slap the third into your empty strong hand (left).

HOT TIP

As always, count out loud, and remember the first two balls go right behind each other. There are two balls in the air at any one time! Yeah, it's harder than the normal cascade, but it's the way most people try to learn without the aid of this book—so it's got to be done. Don't forget to try it the other way round, too!

Two Classic Three-Ball Tricks

The Statue Of Liberty

THIS IS a variation of the shower. Raise your weaker hand, arm straight, rather like the pose of the Statue of Liberty in New York harbor. Now throw a ball from your strong hand up to that hand catching it palm up (below). The hand should be tilted inward, to tip the ball down again, so the other hand can catch it, waist high. Build up with a ball in each hand (below), leading to a shower with three balls.

HOT TIP

The raised hand should hardly move; concentrate on those throws!

GETTING FANCY

Overhead

Find a space with a bit of headroom. lean back your head, and, with a ball in your strong hand, palm up, hand raised to shoulder height, push the ball up and over to the other hand. The catching hand must be in the same position as the throwing hand. Now build up the trick with two balls, and finally three (above).

HOT TIP
If the balls constantly go forward, tip your head back more to compensate.

Having a Three-Ball Ball

A Fancy Start

YOU CAN juggle three balls with ease and confidently put in a few tricks, so what about an impressive way to start a pattern?

1. Take two balls in your strong hand—this time they should rest alongside each other, not one in front of the other (below).
2. Throw them in the air at the same time, so they split up and rise, both to the same height (right).
3. As both balls peak in their arc, the third ball in the other hand is thrown up between them (right), as in the *one-up, two-up* pattern.
4. The two balls are caught with a delay (far right), like in One up, Two up, and then the third ball is included in a three-ball cascade.

GETTING FANCY

HOT TIP
When throwing the two balls together, roll them off the hand, either side of the middle finger, which splits them apart so that the next throw can come up the middle.

To make this trick more dramatic, you can hide the first throw by bringing your other arm horizontally across your body (right), hiding the throwing hand.

The Neck Catch

SO YOU have a start, now you need a flashy finish. The neck catch is the most impressive.

1. Throw a high throw (not too high at first) and bend your body forward from the waist.
2. With the other balls, one in each hand, push your arms out to the sides (below). This should form a "V" shape with your head up and facing forward.
3. The ball will be trapped as it falls into a nice dip, made by your shoulder blades and head —the shoulders will funnel the ball into exactly the right position (right).

GETTING FANCY

HOT TIP
The ball should be thrown vertically and <u>not</u> behind you. Your head tips forward to meet the ball as it drops.

You can go back into the three-ball cascade from here, by dipping your head down and quickly flicking it back up, which in turn flicks the ball up and back into the pattern.

Using the Body

AS WITH all the tricks you have learned so far, try this with just one ball first. Popping a ball off some part of your body is fun and makes for an impressive trick. The easiest option is to bounce a ball off your knee. Throw a normal arc, bring your knee up, and fire the ball back to the original hand (right). With practice, this can be done with any part of the body (below): the elbow, wrist, foot, forehead, whatever. My favorite—after a high throw, gather up the bottom of your T-shirt with both hands, then catch, and "trampoline" the ball back into the pattern.

GETTING FANCY

Stage 4

THERE'S MORE TO LIFE THAN THREE BALLS

Crazy for Numbers

I THINK JUGGLING large numbers of objects is overrated, but that's because I can't do it! The world record for juggling balls is 11. Me, I stick at five.

Four Balls

When juggling two balls in one hand, you learned to throw counterclockwise with the left hand and clockwise with the right (see pages 34–35). To juggle that fourth ball, just throw two balls in both hands (top left, page 53)! Don't the balls cross over? No, both sides stay in the plane of their own sheet of glass.

HOT TIP

Make sure first that you are solid, juggling two balls with your weak hand. If the balls tend to cross, juggle with your hands either side of an open door; wayward balls hit the door and go back into the pattern!

The hands can either throw in-sync or out-of-sync, making columns or circular patterns. Four ways to juggle four balls!

Five Balls

1. Have five balls of the same size and weight.

THERE'S MORE TO LIFE THAN THREE BALLS

2. Place three in your stronger hand, and two in the other.
3. The balls cross as a normal cascade, only slightly higher to give extra time to deal with them (top right). All the normal rules apply: count out loud, stay in the jugglespace, etc. Try just throwing the balls without catching them, and they should land on the floor in two neat clusters of three and two.

HOT TIP

Learn standing over a bed: there will be a lot more drops than normal, so save your back! Don't panic—the pattern is always slower than you think. Your muscles will build up to maintain the rhythm and consistent throws needed to master this routine.

Juggling with Clubs

YOU WILL have seen people juggling with clubs—a lot of people into performance, competition, and social juggling use them. That's because juggling with clubs looks large and impressive. Unfortunately, you have to learn to juggle all over again. Don't believe me? Pick up a set of clubs and give it a whirl. Ouch!

We now have to learn to spin an object. A club is a clever thing. It's big opposite the handle, so that as it spins about its center of gravity (about two-thirds of the way down), the clubhead, misses the catching hand, avoiding injury, presenting the handle to be caught easily.

First hold the club in your strong hand (below left), near the top of

the handle, not right at the knob end. Give it a few spins to the same hand and get the feel of how it performs (bottom right, page 54). Bulbous clubs tend to spin slower.

Now take a look at your hand: palm up, thumb at right angles to the index finger. The club must be caught across the palm, so the fingers can close on the handle. I know that sounds so obvious, but it's not the same as juggling with balls. When you flip it to the other hand, the club should point out to the side of the body at the angle made by the position of the hand, palm up, with the elbows at the side in a relaxed, juggling stance. To achieve this, when throwing the club, sweep it down and throw across your lower body (below left)—this presents it neatly into the waiting hand (below right).

Juggling with Clubs

FOR THE next step, you have a choice. Some say "take two clubs" and follow the rules as in two balls. I recommend that you take one club and one ball and concentrate on making accurate throws with the club (below).

Once you are proficient, you can add either the third club or the second ball (below). If you chose the ball method, then, after you have practiced for some time (right inset), replace each ball with a club (right).

THERE'S MORE TO LIFE THAN THREE BALLS

HOT TIP
If you try to throw the club in the same arc as a ball, you may end up having to twist your hand through 90 degrees to catch it. OK for the odd catch but not every one!

Juggling with Rings

JUGGLING WITH RINGS look very good visually—some people find them better for high-numbers juggling, and they have special tricks of their own.

Rings, like clubs, require a different way of catching and throwing. Grip the ring in your hand with your thumb on top (below). Throw it to your strong hand, dipping the hand down, and releasing the ring with your palm up. Catch it with your palm up and your thumb and index finger facing back toward you (below). Then follow the same sequence as for learning club juggling (right).

HOT TIP
To avoid collisions, the ring must be thrown without any twists, turns, or wobbles in their flight. A good throw with a bit of spin on it is what is required.

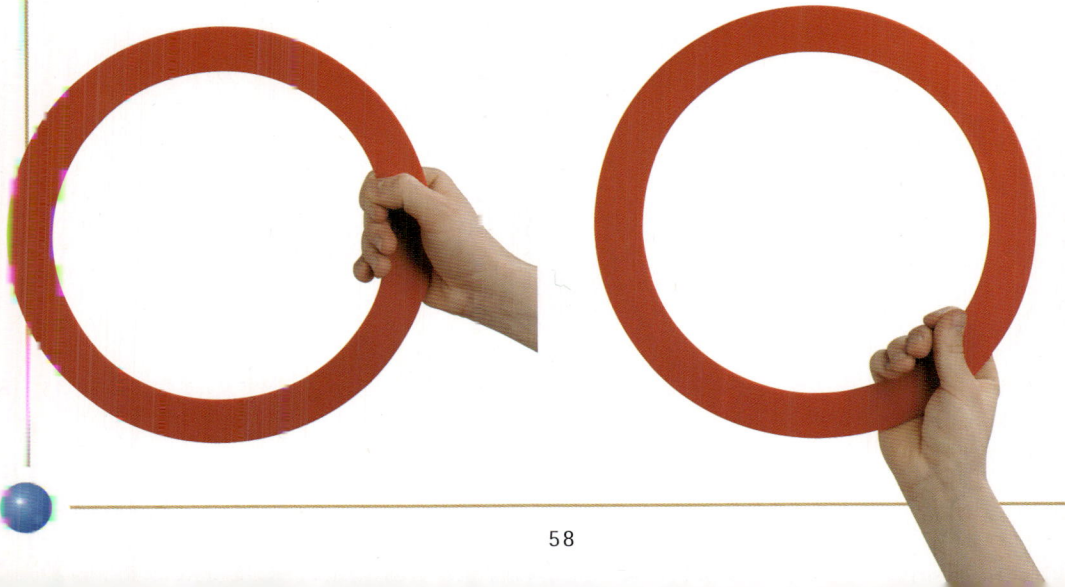

THERE'S MORE TO LIFE THAN THREE BALLS

How to Juggle with Anything

IF YOU have learned the three styles of juggling—balls, clubs, and rings—you can juggle absolutely anything. You just have to work out which of the three styles is appropriate to the object you have chosen. It helps to get used to juggling things that are a mixture of different weights—if you followed my advice by learning clubs and balls mixed, you will already be halfway there.

Here are some hints, although obviously the list is endless. The shape of the object usually gives it away.

Fruits and vegetables: a cucumber or a banana is a club; just about anything else is a ball.
Kitchen implements: those with handles are clubs; plates are rings. Special juggling knives are carefully balanced so it's *not* a

good idea to use the ordinary kitchen variety for juggling, unless you too are very sharp—mistakes can hurt (ouch!).

Tennis rackets, guitars, umbrellas: ...and other long things are all clubs. We talked about the center of gravity, when we learned about clubs (see pages 54–55): objects with a center of gravity, about two-thirds of the way along from the catching end, juggle best.

Scarves: juggling silk scarves (above) can be very graceful. You treat them like balls (but you throw them higher because they spend longer in the air); you have to snatch them, instead of catching them normally.

Frisbees, tires, wheels: rings, of course.

This book: it's a ring, isn't it? It might help if you taped the cover together so it doesn't flap about. Then off you go!

Put the Book Down!

YOU HAVE finished this book, but there is much much, more that you can learn about juggling, and lots of places to find out. The best source is other jugglers. Many cities have juggling workshops that meet weekly, where people swap tricks and ideas. Universities and colleges are often good places to start looking. If there isn't a workshop or club

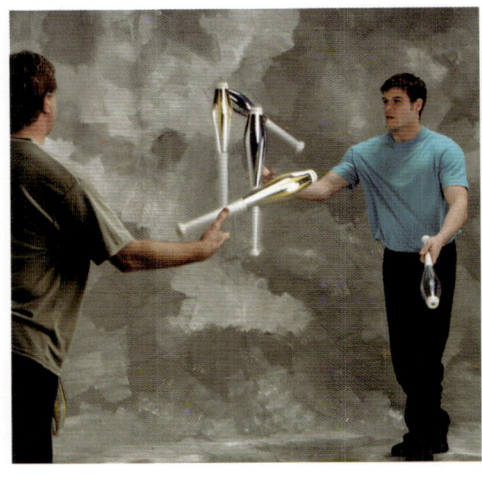

in your town, get a few friends together, and start one!

Every year there are juggling conventions throughout the US and Europe, including big national and international ones, where hundreds or even thousands of jugglers of all abilities meet to have fun and maybe throw a few things in the air, too. There are also many local city conventions. A good place to find out about these is The Juggling Information Service,

THERE'S MORE TO LIFE THAN THREE BALLS

which is on the Internet at www.juggling.org, where you will also find interesting links and places to meet other jugglers online.

One of the most sociable things jugglers do is club passing: two or more people making a juggling pattern together. It's too big a subject to start with in this book, but it is pretty easy to pick up with a few friends. On the net, a lot of jugglers communicate about patterns in a special notation called siteswap. Basically it describes each throw by a number that corresponds to how many balls you'd be juggling if every throw were like that: the three-ball cascade is 333, not throwing a ball is 0. You'll find a more complete explanation online.

Founded in 1947, the International Jugglers Association is a non-profit organization uniquely dedicated to the advancement and promotion of juggling worldwide. IJA membership spans the range from amateur hobbyists to full-time working professionals.
For membership inquiries contact:
IJA Secretary
P.O.Box 218,
Montague, MA 01351 USA
tel (413)-367-2401
fax (413)-367-0259

Further Reading

IF YOUR appetite for juggling books has been whetted by our little volume, you can find more tricks than you would ever want to learn in Charlie Dancey's *Encyclopedia of Ball Juggling* and his *Compendium of Club Juggling*.

Juggle magazine is an invaluable source of information—a subscription to it is one of the benefits of membership the IJA (see page 63).

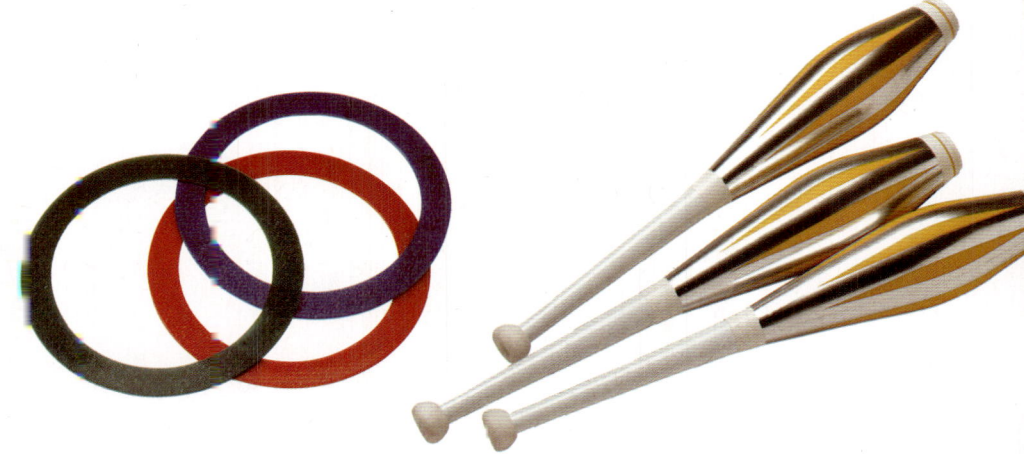

WHO IS THIS JESUS:
IS HE RISEN?

BOOKS BY D. JAMES KENNEDY

Back to Basics
Beginning Again
Character & Destiny
Delighting God
Evangelism Explosion
The Gates of Hell Shall Not Prevail
God's Absolute Best For You
Help, God, I Hurt
How Do I Live for God?
Foundations for Your Faith
Led by the Carpenter
Messiah: Prophecies Fulfilled
New Every Morning
Secrets of Successful Marriage
Skeptics Answered
The Real Meaning of the Zodiac
The Secret to a Happy Home
Solving Bible Mysteries
Truth for Lies
Truths That Transform
Turn It to Gold
What If Jesus Had Never Been Born?
What If the Bible Had Never Been Written?
Why I Believe
Wolves Among Us

WHO IS THIS JESUS: IS HE RISEN?

by

D. James Kennedy, Ph.D.
with
Jerry Newcombe, D.Min.

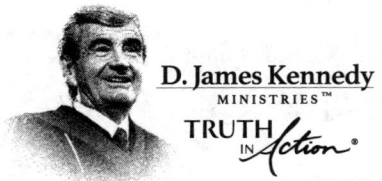

Fort Lauderdale, FL

Who Is This Jesus: Is He Risen?
By D. James Kennedy, Ph.D. with Jerry Newcombe, D.Min.

© 2015 by D. James Kennedy Ministries

All rights reserved. Written permission must be secured from the publisher to use or reproduce any part of this book, except for brief quotations in critical review or articles.

Published by Coral Ridge Ministries
Printed in the United States of America

Transcript of television special, *Who Is This Jesus: Is He Risen?*, © 2001 Coral Ridge Ministries Media, Inc.

Unless otherwise noted all Scripture quotations are from the NEW KING JAMES VERSION. Copyright © 1979, 1980, 1982, Thomas Nelson, Inc., Publishers.

ISBN: 978-1-929626-40-3

Cover and Interior Design: Roark Creative, www.roarkcreative.com

Published by D. James Kennedy Ministries

Printed in the United States of America

D. James Kennedy Ministries
P.O. Box 7009
Albert Lea, MN 56007
1-800-988-7884
www.DJamesKennedy.org
letters@TruthInAction.org

CONTENTS

Introduction
1

The Cornerstone of the Christian Faith
4

The Shroud of Turin
21

The Discovery of Never-ending Life
41

Transcript:
Who Is This Jesus: Is He Risen?
52

Endnotes
98

Index
101

This book is dedicated to Him
who was dead
and is now alive forevermore—
Jesus Christ

INTRODUCTION

There is no greater fear than death, except perhaps that of speaking in public. One wag quipped that if that is really the case, it means that at a funeral the corpse is better off than the eulogizer. All levity aside, death is the really great fear in life . . . or is it what follows death? The great news is that for the Christian, we know that Jesus Christ conquered death on our behalf. We know that because He died for us and rose again, we too will rise again eternally. His death and Resurrection are at the heart of our hope, and they are at the heart of our faith.

Yet today, there are many people who don't believe these basic, foundational truths of the Christian Church anymore. We know that is true *outside* the Church, but now, unfortunately, since the rise of liberalism, and since the deadly influence of liberal seminaries, that is quite often true *inside* the Church as well. Men and women who train future would-be ministers of the Gospel do not even believe the Gospel themselves, and yet they dominate many of our most prestigious seminaries.

I should know—I had to sort through all these issues at a seminary where about half the professors believed the Bible to be the Word of God and the other half did not. Unbelief has grabbed some of the liberal denominations by the throat and is slowly destroying them from within, and nowhere is this clearer than at many of the liberal seminaries. My faith was shaken during my first year of seminary because I had a number of unbelievers for professors. Provi¬dentially, those who were believers helped me keep my head above water. In order to spare others from a similar experience, I eventually founded Knox Theological Seminary, so that the Bible would be taught as the inerrant word of God that it is.

Furthermore, these largely *unbelieving* professors are widely touted on the media. They are interviewed regularly at Christmastime and Easter for network specials or for leading news magazines to spew forth their unbelief.

In this age of mass media, when people widely believe what they see and hear on television and read in the news, many Christians are having their faith shaken by the opinions of such men and women. The irony is that the *facts* are on the conservative side. For example, if you truly examine the evidence for the resurrection of Jesus from an objective perspective, the facts are overwhelming that He stepped out of that tomb on that first Easter Sunday morning.

The purpose of this book is to share some of these basic facts. First, we look at the cornerstone of the Christian faith; we take a look at the immutable facts pointing to Christ's resurrection. Then we consider scientific evidence for the resurrection, as seen in the Shroud of Turin. Next, we discuss the practical implications of His resurrection—what difference does it make in our lives? All the difference in the world.

Finally, we have the transcript from our television special, *Who Is This Jesus: Is He Risen?* We had two similar programs— the first was the award-winning program[1]—*Who Is This Jesus?*, which aired Christmastime 2000. Then there was the Easter adaptation of the same program, *Who Is This Jesus: Is He Risen?* Both featured veteran film actor, Dean Jones, and myself. These specials were our response to Peter Jennings' program, *The Search for Jesus* (ABC-TV, June 2000). I for one was very disappointed in the ABC-TV anchor's program and the way the unbelieving side of such important questions was given a huge megaphone, often without a conservative response. What was tragic was that the program needlessly made mincemeat of people's faith— people who were not armed with the facts. This book is geared toward arming you with the facts, and in our special we have more than one perspective presented, but we show you that

Introduction

the overwhelming evidence points to a solid, conservative conclusion.

We conclude this book with the transcript of *Who Is This Jesus: Is He Risen?* which also includes some of the material from the original *Who Is This Jesus?* that had been cut from the Easter version due to broadcast-time limitations.

We pray that God will use this book to strengthen your faith in His resurrected Son. The fact that He has conquered death gives us hope. Though we will one day face death, the King of Terrors need not maintain the same type of icy grip on our hearts as it does for those who don't know Jesus Christ. Thus, we need neither fear delivering the eulogy, nor being its subject matter.

Chapter 1

The Cornerstone of the Christian Faith[2]

*"If in this life only we have hope in Christ,
we are of all men the most pitiable."*

1 Corinthians 15:19

The evidence for the bodily resurrection of Christ is overwhelming. That is to say, the evidence is overwhelming—unless you reject the miraculous a *priori*, before you study the facts. However, that is not a very objective way to approach anything. Christianity is based on a deep foundation—a foundation that cannot be shaken, despite all the attacks against it. The single most important event in Christianity is the resurrection of Christ.

THE CORNERSTONE OF THE CHRISTIAN FAITH

The evidence for the bodily resurrection of Jesus is compelling. Some historians have called it the best-attested event in antiquity. It is an indisputable fact that the disciples of Jesus were emboldened and transformed from scared rabbits into courageous and bold witnesses who could not be hushed up. The Resurrection is so critically important, because it is the cornerstone of the Christian faith. Take away the Resurrection and Christianity crumbles like a house of cards. Some of the liberal denominations have taken it away from their statements of faith (if they have one), and their churches are withering away—for their congregations instinctively know that there is nothing there but froth, and they will not tolerate being deceived. If Christ were not bodily raised from the dead in human history, Christianity would cease to exist.

The historical, bodily resurrection of Christ from the dead is unique among world religions. Confucius died and was buried. Lao-tse wandered off and died with his water buffalo. Buddha rotted with food poisoning. Mohammed died in 632, and his body was cut up and spread all over the near East. *But Jesus rose from the dead!* By that Resurrection from the dead, He demonstrated that He was indeed the Son of God, with power. By His life, by His death, by His resurrection, He declares that He is God. Let us examine now the case for the resurrection of Christ.

THE RELEVANT EVIDENCE

Any case must deal with *all* of the relevant evidence. Therefore, when you are dealing with the resurrection of Christ, we need to look at all the evidence.

It says in Acts that Christ "presented Himself alive after His suffering by many infallible proofs" (Acts 1:3). I want to examine seven pieces of evidence and seven theories that attempt to explain them away.

First, there is the Christian Church, which is the largest institution or organization that has ever existed on the face of the earth, with membership easily passing two billion people by the end of this decade. Nothing comparable or even close has ever existed before. The Grand Canyon was not caused by an Indian dragging a stick, and the Christian Church wasn't created by a myth.

Historians—secular unbelieving historians—tell us that the Christian Church began in Jerusalem in 30 A.D., the year Christ was killed, and that she began because the apostles began to preach that Jesus Christ rose from the dead. You strip everything else away from their preaching, and their main message was that Christ rose from the dead (e.g., Acts 2:23, 24).

Second, there is the empty tomb. Again, adherents to many religions can travel to the place where the founder of their religion is currently entombed and say, "Here lies the dust of our estimable founder." You cannot say that about Christ. He is not in the grave. He is risen.

For 1,700 years there was virtually no controversy that the tomb was empty. The Jews didn't deny it. The Romans didn't deny it. Nobody denied it until just recently. With our vast "rear view mirror" wisdom, we look back through more than 1,900 years and we decide, "Oh, the tomb wasn't empty." Too bad those who were there couldn't have been so smart.

Third, there is the Roman seal. The huge rock had a rope stretched across it; the clay was fastened to the rope and to the wall of the tomb, and the Roman seal was impressed upon it. If you broke that, you broke the seal. If you broke the seal, you "incurred the wrath of Roman law."[3] The penalty was death.

Fourth, there was the Roman guard. According to Professor Harold Smith, "A Watch usually consisted of four men, each of whom watched in turn, while the others rested beside him so as to be roused by the least alarm; but in this case the guard may have been more numerous."[4] These Roman soldiers were well trained. These people were experts in what they did. The penalty for leaving their post or for falling asleep at the job was death[5]—death that was "always rigorously enforced."[6]

Fifth, there was the stone—at least two tons—probably more. The opening would indicate that the stone would have to be at least about seven or eight feet high. It took more than one person to move it.

Sixth, there were Christ's post-resurrection appearances. These are crucial. He appeared to one, then to another, then to two, then

The Cornerstone of the Christian Faith

to three and then to eight and ten and eleven and 500 people at a time, over a period of about six weeks (1 Corinthians 15:4 9). They saw Him, they heard Him, and they handled Him. He fixed breakfast for them. He ate fish with them (John 21:7 15; Luke 24:42 43).

Connected to the appearances was the transformation of the apostles. One day they were cringing in an upper room for fear of the Jews, and soon after they were boldly upbraiding the Sanhedrin and proclaiming the resurrection of Christ. Consider also their martyrdom. They were crucified (crucified upside down), sawed in half, stoned to death, and killed in many other ways—all except John, who was exiled to the island of Patmos by Nero. Why would they give their lives for what they *knew* to be false?

Seven, there is the character of Christ Himself. Christ is universally acknowledged, even often enough by skeptics, to be a paragon of virtue, the most noble, moral, truthful, and ethical man the world has ever seen. The last thing Jesus would promote would be deception, including the deception that He rose from the dead—if, in fact, He did not.

THEORIES THAT TRY TO EXPLAIN AWAY THE RESURRECTION OF CHRIST

As apologist Josh McDowell points out, some theories to explain away the resurrection of Christ take as much faith to believe as the Resurrection itself.[7] He has debated the Resurrection with skeptics more than just about anybody alive. He writes:

> After more than 700 hours of studying this subject and thoroughly investigating its foundation, I have come to the conclusion that the resurrection of Jesus Christ is one of the *most wicked, vicious, heartless hoaxes ever foisted upon the minds of men,* or it is the most fantastic fact of history ... A student at the University of Uruguay said to me: "Professor

McDowell, why can't you refute Christianity?" I answered: "For a very simple reason I am not able to explain away an event in history—the resurrection of Jesus Christ."[8]

Let's examine now some of the theories put forth to explain away the resurrection of Jesus Christ.

THE FRAUD THEORY

The first theory—which was and is the theory of the Jews—to explain away Christ's resurrection is the Fraud Theory. Essentially, what the Jews are saying is that the whole thing was a fraud. We read: "Now while they were going, behold, some of the guard came into the city and reported to the chief priests all the things that had happened" (Matthew 28:11).

Interestingly, you hear it said sometimes that Jesus never appeared to anybody but believers, but it is not true. He appeared to the guards. They were so terrified by His appearance that they fainted and became as dead men. Then they came and told the high priest what had happened. Jesus appeared to James, his brother, who was skeptical. Jesus appeared to Saul, the persecutor. These people were not Christians at the time.

The Bible continues: "When they had assembled with the elders and consulted together, they gave a large sum of money to the soldiers, saying, 'Tell them His disciples came at night and stole Him away while we slept. And if this comes to the governor's ears, we will appease him and make you secure.' So they took the money and did as they were instructed; and this saying is commonly reported among the Jews until this day" (Matthew 28:12-15) . . . even until this day, nearly 2,000 years later.

Let's consider how that stacks up with the evidence. First of all, there is the Christian Church. Does the Fraud Theory give a plausible reason for the Christian Church? The Church was founded by the apostles who preached the Resurrection. If the Fraud Theory were right, then they knew they had stolen the body and planted it in the rose garden, but they went ahead and proclaimed that He had risen from the dead.

Something happened to the disciples that changed them in a moment from cowardice to heroic courage. They said it was that they had seen Jesus risen from the dead. To say that they stole the body and made up a resurrection does not make sense. That view does not reflect the realities of human nature. For example, when two criminals are charged with the same murder, even when they have previously been friends, they will almost invariably accuse the other of pulling the trigger. But the disciples did not change their story one bit, although they had everything to gain and nothing to lose by doing so! The apostles continued throughout all of their lives to proclaim that they had seen Him risen from the dead. Their speaking out led to torture and execution, but none of them ever sought to save his own skin by revealing the "plot."

Dr. Principal Hill, who wrote *Lectures in Divinity*, which were popular in the 19th century, has shown the absurdity of the Fraud Theory perhaps more succinctly than anyone else. This is terrific:

> You must suppose that twelve men of mean birth, of no education, living in that humble station which placed ambitious views out of their reach and far from their thoughts, without any aid from the state, formed the noblest scheme which ever entered into the mind of man, adopted the most daring means of executing that scheme, conducted it with such address as to conceal the imposture under the semblance of simplicity and virtue. You must suppose, also, that men guilty of blasphemy and falsehood, united in an attempt the best contrived, and which has in fact proved the most successful for making the world virtuous; that they formed this single enterprise without seeking any advantage to themselves, with an avowed contempt of loss and profit, and with the certain expectation of scorn and persecution; that although conscious of one another's villainy, none of them ever thought of providing for his own security by disclosing the fraud, but that amidst sufferings the most grievous to flesh and blood they persevered in their conspiracy to *cheat* the world into

piety, honesty and benevolence. Truly, they who can swallow such suppositions have no title to object to miracles.[9]

How true that is. No, the Fraud Theory will not stand up to the evidence.

THE SWOON THEORY

A second theory to explain away the Resurrection is the Swoon Theory. This is the theory of the Christian Scientists. The Swoon Theory is the idea that Jesus never really died. It is interesting that until the 1800s, nobody ever thought that Jesus had not died. Everybody believed He had.

I think it is significant that the people who put Him to death were "in the business." What was their trade? Their business was taking people who were alive and making them into people who were dead. That is what they did for a living. They would go home at night and say, "Well, I did three today, honey." They were experts at what they did.

But what the Swoon Theory says is that Jesus did not really die; He merely swooned and then, being placed in the fresh coolness of the tomb, He revived. That does not live up to the facts. Obviously, here is a man who had been scourged, which often killed people in and of itself. His hands and feet and His side had been pierced.

In the Philippines, some people have had themselves crucified on Good Friday. They will sometimes stay up there for three, four, or five minutes, and then—not having been scourged, not having been up all night, not having gone without food for hours, not having had their side and pericardium pierced—they are taken down and to the hospital, where they very nearly die!

Jesus, we are supposed to believe, having been placed in the cool freshness of a tomb, revived. But if a person has gone into shock, should you put him in a cool place? No way. That would kill him. Instead, you cover him with blankets and try to keep his body temperature up. So, the cool freshness of the tomb may sound nice on a hot day, but if you are in shock that is the last thing you want. In fact, if He were not dead when they put Him into the tomb, that most certainly would have killed Him.[10]

Supposedly, He stays there for three days, and then He gets up on mangled feet, hobbles to the door of the tomb and finds this stone weighing a few tons. He places His mangled hands against the flat side of the rock and rolls it away, overcomes the Roman guard of armed men, and takes a seven-mile hike to Emmaus chatting with the fellows on the way. No one noticed He was limping! Then He treks almost a hundred miles to Galilee, climbs a mountain, and there He convinces 500 people that He is the Lord of Life!

The Swoon Theory has received a fatal blow from a skeptic by the name of David Friedrich Strauss—a nineteenth century German who wrote a life of Christ. He didn't believe in the Resurrection, but he knew the Swoon Theory was utterly ridiculous. Listen to what an unbeliever says about this:

> It is impossible that a being who had stolen half dead out of the sepulcher, who crept about, weak and ill, wanting medical treatment, who required bandaging, strengthening, and indulgence, and who, still at last, yielded to his sufferings, could have given to the disciples the impression that he was a conqueror over death and the grave, The Prince of Life, an impression which lay at the bottom of all of their future ministry—such a resuscitation could only have weakened the impression which he made in life and in death and at the most, could only have given it an elegiac voice, a lament for the dead. But could by no possibility have changed their sorrow into enthusiasm, have elevated their reverence into worship.[11]

And with Strauss' critique, for those other than the devoted Christian Scientists, the Swoon Theory has swooned away.

THE SPIRITUAL RESURRECTION THEORY

Then there is the view of the Jehovah's Witnesses, which is the Spiritual Resurrection Theory. This theory also seems to be gaining currency with some theological liberals today. They say that Jesus' resurrection was not physical, but spiritual, and that He was just a spirit. The Bible directly refutes this:

"Now as they said these things, Jesus Himself stood in the midst of them, and said to them, 'Peace to you.' But they were terrified and frightened, and supposed they had seen a spirit" (Luke 24:36-37).

Yes, says the Jehovah's Witnesses, they were right. What they saw was a spirit. Not so fast. Luke continues:

> And He said to them, "Why are you troubled? And why do doubts arise in your hearts? Behold My hands and My feet, that it is I Myself. Handle Me and see, for a spirit does not have flesh and bones as you see I have." When He had said this, He showed them His hands and His feet. But while they still did not believe for joy, and marveled, He said to them, "Have you any food here?" So they gave Him a piece of broiled fish and some honeycomb. And He took it and ate in their presence (Luke 24:38-43).

This is not to mention the fact that if Jesus were just a ghost or spirit, then what about the body? Well, the body is still in the tomb. What about the disciples who ran to the tomb when they heard that Jesus had risen? They would have gotten there, and the stone would be in front of the door, and Jesus would still be in the tomb. Well, the Jehovah's Witnesses have managed to take care of that, too, with the same disregard of anything the Scripture or history teaches, and they simply say that God destroyed the body. He evaporated it, so it just disappeared, but there is nothing in the Bible that says anything whatsoever about that.

THE WRONG PERSON THEORY

Fourth, there is the view of the Muslims. This is the Wrong Person Theory. I doubt very much if you ever heard of this because, other than the Muslims, I don't know of anybody that believes it. But the Koran says of Jesus, "They slew him not nor crucified, but it appeared so unto them" (Surah 4:157). They believe that somehow, on Good Friday, there was a mix-up and Judas got crucified. The eyewitness accounts say that Jesus was crucified. Second, we have Mary, His mother, standing at the foot of the Cross for all of those hours looking at Him and weeping over her dying son. He says to her, "Mother."

According to this theory, she was confused—as were Pilate, the Sanhedrin, and the disciples. Everybody was confused, including Jesus—because He then came to the disciples after He rose from the dead. I wonder who they think appeared to the disciples and said, "Behold my hands and feet?" Do they believe that Judas arose from the dead? They have the same kind of problem they tried to get rid of—somebody that God raised from the dead, which He didn't do with Mohammed.

Another fatal flaw to this theory is that it doesn't coincide at all with the *character* of Jesus. He was a man of impeccable integrity, but according to this theory, He would be a fraud, a deceiver. Furthermore, if this theory were true, then the tomb would still be occupied (but we know it's empty); Judas' body would still be in the tomb. What about the guards? What happened to them? When the early Christians declared Jesus had risen from the dead, they could have easily countered what they said and just showed them the tomb with the Roman seal still affixed. This theory doesn't fit any of the known facts in this case.

THE HALLUCINATION THEORY

Fifth, there is the Hallucination Theory, which claims that all of the disciples simply had hallucinations when they saw

Him risen from the dead. Psychologists have pointed out that hallucinations are idiosyncratic[12]—that is, they are very personal and private, and people don't have collective hallucinations. Jesus appeared to the people in the morning; He fixed breakfast with them. They hallucinated having breakfast. He appeared at noon, He walked with them to Emmaus, He appeared with them at suppertime several times, He appeared inside; He appeared outside. He even appeared to 500 people at one time. Not only did they see Him, but also they heard Him, talked to Him, handled Him, and watched Him eat. They could not have been hallucinating these things, not to mention the other evidence. Having thus hallucinated that Jesus was alive and had appeared to them, they ran to the tomb and hallucinated that the tomb was empty, the guard was gone, the stone was rolled away, and the grave clothes were empty. Then they began to preach that Jesus rose from the dead. If that were the case, this hallucination would be contagious. They declared that "You, Sanhedrin, you have taken with wicked hands and you have slain the Prince of Life and Glory and God has raised Him from the dead." So, the Sanhedrin ran down to the tomb and had the same hallucination—that it was empty, too.

The Romans, seeing there was a tumult, went down and checked things out and talked to the guards. The guards all had hallucinations that the tomb was empty. This is all ridiculous, obviously. It doesn't deal with any of the evidence.

THE WRONG TOMB THEORY

There is the theory that suggests the women went to the wrong tomb. Again, we must deal with the evidence. It is conceivable that the women got mixed up, and though they had been there on Friday evening, they went to the wrong tomb. According to Kirsopp Lake, a liberal biblical scholar who taught at Harvard (1914-37), this was conceivable in that there were so many tombs around Jerusalem. But I've been to that tomb, and there aren't any tombs around it. Nor were there at the time of Christ.

If this theory were correct, the women went to the wrong tomb, Peter and John (by themselves) ran to the wrong tomb, and the disciples went to the wrong tomb. Joseph of Arimathea, who owned the tomb, naturally would want to see what happened, and yet he, too, went to the wrong tomb. The Sanhedrin also was concerned and went to the wrong tomb. Then, of course, the angel came down, and the angel went to the wrong tomb—for what does an angel know about tombs?

Of course, all the while there were the guards saying, "Hey, fellows, we're over here!" They, at least, were at the right tomb. Again, this is obviously is a wrong theory, and it doesn't answer any of the facts.

If the women and everybody else went to the wrong tomb and started proclaiming Christ risen from the dead, what would the Sanhedrin do? It would go to the right tomb, tell the soldiers to roll back the stone and say, "Bring Him out." Then it would hang His corpse up by the heels in the town square in Jerusalem, and say, "There is your glorious Prince of Life! Take a good whiff of His rotting corpse." That would have been the end of Christianity right then and there.

THE LEGEND THEORY

Lastly, there is the Legend Theory. This is the idea that the "myth" of Christ rising from the dead just sort of gradually grew up over the decades and centuries. This view was popular in the nineteenth century. That was back when they said that the Gospels were written in the second or even the third century, by people other than the apostles, but all of that has collapsed in the last 30 or 40 years. Even the late Bishop John A. T. Robinson, of England, one of the most blatant critics, wrote a book pointing out that the conservative scholars were right all along and that the Gospels were written by the men whose names they bear and in the times we have said they were written. Robinson said, near the end of his life, that he believed all the Gospels, including John, were written before 70 A.D.[13]

Furthermore, as stated above, secular historians point out that the Church of Jesus Christ began in 30 A.D. in Jerusalem, because the apostles preached the Resurrection. Jesus and the Resurrection were the central thrust of their teaching. So there was no time for myth making or legend spinning. As Peter said, "For we did not follow cunningly devised fables when we made known to you the power and coming of our Lord Jesus Christ, but were eyewitnesses of His majesty" (2 Peter 1:16). John said, speaking of Jesus: "That which was from the beginning, which we have heard, which we have seen with our eyes, which we have looked upon, and our hands have handled, concerning the Word of life . . . we declare to you" (1 John 1:1, 3b).

What is more, we know how all of the apostles died. They were crucified and stoned and cut up. All this was done to them . . . supposedly for believing a legend which had not even yet developed, which was not going to develop for another 100 or 150 years. That is absurd. It doesn't deal with any of the factual information. It doesn't deal with what the Sanhedrin, the Jews and the Romans would have done.

In his book, *The Historical Jesus*, Gary Habermas points out that there are 18 different first or second century pagan (or at least non-Christian) writers, who present more than a hundred facts about the birth of Christ, His life, teachings, miracles, crucifixion, resurrection and ascension. These names are listed in the transcript of our television special. They include Josephus, Tacitus, Thallus, Phlegon, Pliny the Younger, Suetonius, Emperor Trajan, Emperor Hadrian, the Talmud, Lucian, Mara Bar-Serapion, and so on.[14] This is no legend that was built up over the centuries.

"MIRACLES DON'T HAPPEN"

Some people begin with the assumption that miracles don't happen; therefore, Christ could not have risen from the dead. This doesn't explain any of the facts. This is also circular logic. It is merely a presupposition that disallows the possibility of the Resurrection. Who is open minded in this instance? Surely not those who reject the Resurrection out of hand because they know miracles don't happen. How can anyone know that miracles don't happen? That is an illogical assumption.

BUT CHRIST HAS RISEN FROM THE DEAD

The truth is that Christ did rise from the dead. The greatest problem mankind has ever faced, generation after generation, century after century, millennia after millennia, has been solved by Jesus. Death has been with us since the fall of man, and always people have asked, "If a man dies, will he rise again?" Jesus Christ has given us irrefutable evidence that the answer is "Yes." The greatest efforts of the most brilliant, unbelieving skeptical minds of the last 2,000 years to disprove the Resurrection have all come to naught. There is not one of them that could stay afloat in a debate for 15 minutes when the evidence is given a fair examination.

There are other evidences I could discuss at length if space permitted. I will mention one more briefly. Most notable is the transformation of the Sabbath from the Jewish Saturday to the Christian Sunday. The Resurrection took place amidst Jews who were committed and zealous Sabbatarians. How is it that suddenly the Christian Church changed from the seventh day Sabbath to the first day? Because the resurrection of Jesus Christ from the dead happened on the first day of the week. For these Jews who believed in Jesus, and all the early Christians were Jews, to switch over from strict observance of Saturday as their holy Sabbath to Sunday as the all-important "Lord's day," as it is called in the New

Testament, was a monumental shift. The Resurrection was the cause of that shift. Christians have been worshiping Jesus Christ on Sunday from the very beginning until the present.

CONCLUSION

The Apostle Paul had to deal with a first century false teaching going around in the Church at Corinth. Some of the members of that Church were claiming that there was no resurrection of the dead, which would imply that Jesus had not risen from the dead. Paul then wrote the following words, which have assured tens of millions of Christians down through the centuries: "And if Christ is not risen, then our preaching is empty and your faith is also empty. . . .

And if Christ is not risen, your faith is futile; you are still in your sins! Then also those who have fallen asleep in Christ have perished. If in this life only we have hope in Christ, we are of all men the most pitiable. But now Christ is risen from the dead, and has become the firstfruits of those who have fallen asleep" (1 Corinthians 15:14, 17 20).

Chapter 2

The Shroud of Turin

"And she brought forth her firstborn Son, and wrapped Him in swaddling cloths, and laid him in a manger; because there was no room for them in the inn."

—Luke 2:7

On Christmas morning, in millions of homes around the country, ribbons, bows, and wrappings of all sorts will be flying around in profusion, as eager young people commit mayhem on carefully wrapped and beribboned packages. Now and again there will be found under the tree a package that has been wrapped beautifully and so delightfully that someone might say, "Wait, save that wrapping. Save it for possible future use." I am sure we have all seen that happen at one time or another. The wrappings are just too beautiful and too valuable to throw away.

Another thing that happens at Christmastime is that some people do not like what they have received, so after Christmas they line up to take the gifts back, just as they lined up to buy them in the first place. Of course, by then the ribbons and wrappings have all been torn up. They are not wrapped up neatly, but usually are shoved in some old brown paper bag and taken back to the store.

Ribbons and wrapping are so much a part of our Christmas tradition. As I thought about this, it occurred to me that maybe there is a "word" in the wrappings. Could there be? If so, what might that be?

As I searched the Scriptures, I noted that God's great Christmas gift to mankind, His own Son, was wrapped. We are told: "And she brought forth her firstborn Son and wrapped in swaddling cloths." So, before being presented to the world, God's Christmas gift also was wrapped. In thinking further on this, it came to me that the world did not like the Christmas gift from God and sent it back. Most people, however, have the courtesy and good taste to not have damaged the presents they take back to the store. God's Christmas gift, however, was used, bruised, and abused before it was sent back. Interestingly, we find that it, too, was wrapped before it was returned. We read that Joseph of Arimathea wrapped Him in a clean linen cloth.

Fascinatingly, the claim has been made for some time that the wrapping in which the gift of God was sent back to Heaven has been saved. I speak of what is known as the Shroud of Turin, which many claim is the actual burial shroud provided by Joseph of Arimathea, in which the body of Jesus was wrapped before burial. That wrapping has been subjected to the most intensive scientific scrutiny ever placed upon any religious artifact in history.

There is indeed a word in the wrappings. Is this wrapping actually the burial shroud of Christ, or is it some sort of pious hoax perpetrated by a medieval artist? It is worth our examining today. We have seen that Jesus came and was born into the world. He was born in a manger and He went to a Cross. Is this shroud real? Is there further evidence that has been attested by science confirming the message of the Bible given us? Is this a fraud?

I should confess that when I first heard about the so-called Shroud of Turin, my attitude was one of great skepticism. I have never been impressed with relics. There are enough pieces of the "genuine" cross of Christ to build the ark, and there are at least forty other shrouds that are claimed to be the Shroud of Christ. Was this any different? I, for one, did not think so at all. However, it should be required of every honest person—certainly of every Christian—to have an open mind and to examine the evidence. Christianity is based upon evidence. What does the evidence say? It was with interest that I heard about the earlier photographic examinations that had been made by some Italian scientists.

In 1978 the Shroud of Turin Research Project was formed. The group was composed of thirty-three scientists, most of them Americans who came from the space research laboratories, from computer analyses, from every type of microscopic, spectroscopic, photographic, and analytical discipline. They sought permission to scientifically scrutinize the Shroud as no religious artifact had ever been examined before.

HISTORICAL FACTS ABOUT THE SHROUD OF TURIN

Before I tell you what the results were, let me give you the history of the Shroud and the person whose image is indelibly affixed to it. The Shroud of Turin can be positively traced back to 1357 when it was displayed for the first time in Lirey, France, by the house of Geoffrey de Charny. When it was displayed, the bishop of the area was incensed at the idea of some middle class family in his area actually possessing the genuine shroud of Christ. He stopped the exhibition and refused to have it shown any further.

In 1449 the granddaughter of the deceased de Charny displayed it again. The succeeding bishop again tried to have the exhibition stopped. It was termed to be a fraud. It was said to have been painted by a cunning artist.

There were some "sidonologists" (those who study the Shroud) who believe it can be traced back to about 1000 A.D. in Constantinople and to Edessa, where it may be traced all the way back to the first century. Be that as it may, those connections are very tenuous at best. It has been found that when a pollenologist (one who studies the various spores or pollens produced by seed-bearing plants) examined the pollens that were taken off the

Shroud, there were about forty: five or six of them from France, more from the area of Turkey, and the vast majority of them from Palestine. Furthermore, the Shroud itself was made of linen, but it was microscopically detected that there were pieces of cotton also within, indicating it had been woven on a loom that had also been used to weave cotton. Cotton was not produced in Europe in the Middle Ages, though it was plentiful in the Middle East. Indeed the plot begins to thicken.

THE IMAGE ON THE SHROUD

The Shroud measures three and one half feet wide and fourteen feet long. It was apparently placed under and over the entire body of the man represented in the Shroud, covering him down to his feet. On the Shroud is a minutely detailed and accurate picture of the entire body of this person—both the front and back of the individual, revealing an entire human form. I am sure most of you have seen a picture of that face and that body. The man is lying with his hands folded across the pelvic area.

The image of a man is identified by ethnologists as a Semite, having the features of a Jew. He is approximately 5'10" tall and about 175 pounds in weight. He is a man who has suffered a very violent death. He is unclothed. He has been horribly flogged. Unquestionably, he was flogged with the Roman flagrum, which was a whip of three long pieces of rawhide with a wooden handle. At the end of each piece is a tiny piece of lead shaped like a bow tie and held in the middle with the thong. There are at least a hundred and twenty or more indentations indicated in the Shroud, where every part of the body except the arms, the head, and the feet is covered with these. In this particular case, these pieces of lead were actually sharpened so that they bit more deeply into the flesh.

What we see is a picture of a person who has been terribly flogged and scourged. It is ascertained by the medical examiners who examined the Shroud that this man was flogged by two

The Shroud of Turin

3D enhancement of the Shroud image
Courtesy of Dr. Alan Whanger

individuals who stood on either side of him and alternated blows, one of whom was taller than the other and one of whom scourged him more fiercely and savagely than did the other. The scourging went all the way down to the ankles and up to the neck.

Furthermore, we see that this is a man who has been crowned with thorns—not the usual ringlet depicted in Christian art—that was pressed down on his head, producing innumerable puncture wounds all over the forehead and head, which bled profusely over the face. We note also that part of the beard had been plucked out.

An artist's rendering of the picture on the Shroud produces precisely that traditional picture you see of Jesus. Now, either a cunning craftsman in the fourteenth century put the traditional picture of Jesus on the Shroud or else the Shroud has been the source of the traditional pictures of Jesus that we have known through the centuries. It is one or the other. We will note later (in discussing a sixth century icon) that clearly, the Shroud came first and then our image of what we think Jesus looked like.

We see that the person had been beaten in the face before he was crucified. His left eye is almost swollen shut. He has contusions on his chin and several places on his face. Furthermore, we see that across his shoulders a heavy weight of some sort had been placed because there are abrasions that scrape away the marks left by the scourging. Apparently, he had had a violent fall. There are cuts on both knees and a deep cut on the left knee. Furthermore, the left septum had been violently torn from the face. His nose had been broken, as if he had fallen with no effort to break the fall with his hands.

We also note that the man has been crucified in the feet and hands. The left foot is placed over the right and a single spike has pierced them both. In the case of his hands, the spikes are found at the base of the hand, the beginning of the wrist, between the radius and ulna. It is interesting that traditional Christian art has always shown Christ with the spikes in the palms. Dr. Pierre Barbet, in the early part of the twentieth century, experimented with corpses, actually crucifying them, and found that nails in the palms ripped out easily and were incapable of supporting the weight of a human being.[15]

Further excavations have revealed that other victims of Roman crucifixion were indeed pierced at the base of the hands or the wrist. Furthermore, the Greek word *cheir* and the Hebrew word *yad* both mean "hand," "wrist," or "forearm." Therefore, the Shroud is not contrary to the teaching of the Scriptures, but contrary to the generally accepted view that has been held until recent evidence has shown otherwise.

We further note that the man has been pierced in the right side with a wound that is one and three-fourths inches long and seven-sixteenth of an inch wide, which happens to fit exactly with an extant Roman *lancea*—the lance with a leaf-shaped blade used by Roman centurions. This is, indeed, an amazing coincidence.

We might also note that the legs of this man in the Shroud were not broken, as was the custom. Once his legs were broken, the crucified person could no longer lift himself up, causing the pectoral muscles to become paralyzed. When that happened, he was unable to exhale and was soon asphyxiated. The person was constantly raising himself up on the spike by straightening his knees and then collapsing in agony and continuing to do this all the hours he was on the cross. In the case of the man in the Shroud, there are two streams of blood on the arm, ten degrees apart, showing that he was in both the elevated and the collapsed positions. But his legs were not broken.

These are amazing descriptions, completely in harmony in every single detail of what we know historically and biblically of the death and crucifixion of Christ.

We might also note this: He received a burial according to the Jewish custom, but only in part. He was covered with a shroud, as the Bible says. It also indicated that there was a napkin or cloth placed around his head. Generally, it has been thought that this napkin covered his face. Scientists now believe this was a napkin wrapped into a roll and tied around the head in order to close the mouth. Jewish ritual commands that this be done so rigor mortis would not set in with the person's mouth agape. In fact, there is a separation on the left side of the beard, indicating that something is covering part of the beard, which is believed to be the headband keeping the mouth closed. There is a cloth in Spain, the Sudarium of Oveido, which is believed to be the head cloth used to wrap the face of Christ. Furthermore, scientists have found that the bloodstains on the Sudarium can be matched up with the bloodstains on the Shroud.

It has now been discovered that coins covered the eyes, as was the Jewish custom of that time. These coins had been discovered by the late Father Francis Filas to be leptons that were minted in Judea between A.D. 29 and 31 by Pontius Pilate. Christ was crucified in the year A.D. 30—a remarkable coincidence, indeed.

We can see that the burial was incomplete and that the body was not washed. We know that the Sabbath was coming on, and they had to stop their burial proceedings. The women returned early Sunday morning to complete them, but Jesus had risen from the dead. We find that in all these details the Shroud matches what we have from the Scriptures.

EFFORTS TO DATE THE SHROUD

The question now is: Is it a cunningly devised portrait painted by some clever medieval artist? Wasn't it widely reported in 1988, when they carbon-dated the Shroud that whatever its origin, it dated only from about 1300?

While the carbon dating test in 1988 seemed to indicate the Shroud was of medieval origin, there are many who dispute that test on several reasonable grounds—most notably, they object to where—on the Shroud itself—they selected the samples to test. The 1978 STURP group called for a protocol involving seven samples chosen from various spots around the Shroud. That protocol was violated. Instead, three samples were *all* taken from the *same* spot. Which spot? Perhaps a rewoven part of the cloth. During the Middle Ages, the Shroud was often put on public display. Nuns had sewn parts of the cloth in a way that the Shroud could be held up on its side by several poles. The view here is that the portion of the Shroud used in the dating is not authentically from the Shroud itself, but from one of the rewoven parts of the cloth. Note that there are thousands of scientific tests that argue for the Shroud's authenticity. To my knowledge, one test alone—the carbon dating test—argues that it is a fraud.

Archaeologist William Meacham warned *before* the carbon-14 dating of 1988 to not take such a test too seriously: "There seems to be an unhealthy consensus approaching the level of dogma among both scientists and lay commentators that C-14 dating will settle the issue once and for all time. This attitude simply contradicts the general perspective of field archaeologists and geologists who view contamination as a very serious problem."[16]

Father Joseph Marino, O.S.B., a sindonologist at the Benedictine

Abbey in St. Louis says: " . . . the sample containing the frontal image; this corner is the most contaminated area of the Shroud. This is the area that has been constantly handled whenever the Shroud has been taken out for exhibits and private showings."[17]

Dr. Alan Whanger, retired Duke Medical School professor and respected sindonologist since the late 1970s, and his wife Mary, wrote this about the carbon dating:

> "Contrary to much public opinion, carbon 14 dating is not an exact science. . . . A major reason why obtaining an accurate carbon dating for the Shroud is so difficult is that it has been in the open, moved from place to place, and handled by hundreds of people. Most artifacts, to be dated, have been buried in one spot for thousands of years and are then taken directly to the laboratory. But the Shroud has been in contact with oils, wax, soaps, paints, ointments, open wounds, saliva, sweat, pollens, flowers and other plant parts, organic carbon compounds, microscopical fungi and bacteria, and insect debris."[18]

Carbon-14 dating in general is not always as accurate as many people believe. In his book *The Resurrection of the Shroud*, author Marc Antonacci highlights just a few of the many errors of carbon-14 dating:

- dating of *living* snail shells to be twenty-six thousand years old
- dating a newly killed seal to be thirteen hundred years old
- dating one-year-old leaves as four hundred years old
- dating twenty-six-thousand-year-old-mammoth fur as fifty-six hundred years old
- dating a Viking horn to the future year of 2006.[19]

So we see carbon-14 dating is not always so accurate. Even *TIME* magazine reported in a cover story on the Shroud, ten years after the 1988 carbon dating: "It is obviously within the realm of possibility that the radiocarbon tests on the Shroud of Turin were faulty. . . questions regarding the typicality of the sample swatch cannot be summarily dismissed."[20]

In short, the carbon dating testing which seemed to discredit the Shroud in 1988 as a medieval forgery was blown out of proportion. The media strikes again.

INTENSE STUDY OF THE SHROUD

Almost forty scientists went to Italy in 1978. They brought with them 72 crates of millions of dollars worth of the most sophisticated scientific instruments and for five days, twenty-four hours a day, in shifts, they exposed that Shroud to every conceivable scientific test. They spent three years analyzing their findings. Though many articles have come out at different times, one thing is definite: In reading the findings of this scientific team, it makes very clear that all the previous reports are either incomplete, completely inaccurate, or filled with false information.

For example, their most conclusive finding of all is that there is no pigment, no dye, no ink, no foreign substance of any kind whatsoever that could produce this incredibly detailed figure of the dorsal and frontal aspect of this entire human being. Their most overwhelming conclusive determination is that it was not produced by the application of anything of any sort to the Shroud. There is nothing there, which is an astonishing revelation. Under the most exhaustive, microscopic X-ray and every kind of test, they found nothing there that produces that image.

In fact, what produces the image is what is not there. What is not there is the fact that some of the fibrils of the individual linen threads are dehydrated. It is this dehydrating that produces the yellow tint that produces the picture of the Shroud. Intensities of color are not there. They are all exactly the same. The only difference in tint is due to the fact that in some places there are more dehydrated threads than others. Furthermore, this dehydration is superficial. Each tiny thread is made up of two hundred fibrils and the superficial nature of the imprint is such that it goes only two or three fibrils deep. It has been totally beyond any modern scientific technique known to be able to produce an image on the Shroud which is that superficial. If you turn the Shroud over, there is no image at all.

Thirdly, they discovered when they used the VP-8 Image Analyzer (an analyzer which is used by NASA to examine light from stars and pictures of planets, turning it into three dimensional images), they found that the image on this Shroud turns into a three-dimensional picture of a human being. It is very impressive to see the three-dimensional figure leap out at you. It is interesting that none of the pictures and photographs and paintings of Jesus, when the same analyzer is used, produce a three-dimensional portrait. A portrait of any kind comes off distorted when put through this analyzer—not so with the Shroud of Turin.

In 1898, when the very first picture of it was taken, photographer Secondo Pia discovered that he held a photographic positive in his hands. In 1357, photography had never even been dreamed of, and the concept of negativity and positivity was not even known. Yet, the Shroud of Turin is a photographic negative, so when the first photograph was taken, suddenly, for the first time, the figure leaped out in all its graphic details. It had never been seen that way before.

We find, also, that the image is completely directionless. There is no indication of brushwork upon it. The image is just there. Furthermore, there is no capillary flow. There is no indication of anything ever having been put on it that could have flowed into any of the fibrils or any of the threads, as any substance would tend to do. It is thermally stable, chemically stable, water stable. They have thus concluded that the image was not produced by paint of any sort, by dyes, powders, spices, or any other substances on the Shroud itself.

Furthermore, earlier reports had indicated that what appears to be blood on the Shroud was not blood. One of the conclusions of the new careful and complete examinations is that it is undoubtedly blood.

We find that very interesting conclusions can be drawn. Here was a man who was a Jew, who was first flogged, who was crowned with thorns, and who was crucified by the Romans. We know of no one in history being crucified after first being crowned with thorns and later pierced in the side other than Jesus. We know of no other person whose legs were not broken and whose beard was plucked. When all these factors were computed by probability scientists, the conclusion was that the probabilities were 1 in 225 billion that this was some other person than Jesus of Nazareth. Scientists will never say that this was Jesus. They operate on probabilities, and those are extraordinarily high probabilities. Chemist Alan Adler, who was one of the members of the STURP team that investigated the Shroud so thoroughly in 1978, put it well when he said in *Time* magazine: "Science can never authenticate this cloth, because there's no lab test for Christ-ness."[21]

There are other conclusions that can be reached. In the nineteenth century there was devised a Swoon Theory (already discussed in the previous chapter) which said that Jesus had never died; therefore, He did not rise from the dead, but was simply revived. One thing the scientists have absolutely concluded is that whoever that man in the Shroud was, he was dead. Rigor mortis had already set in. His left knee is bent slightly, where one foot had been placed on top of the other. His head, through rigor mortis, is bent slightly forward. We read in the Scripture that Jesus, having bowed His head, gave up the ghost. We see that medical examiners and coroners, having examined the spear wound in His side, have conclusively determined that the spear passed through the pericardium and also through the heart. There is no doubt about the fact that when that spear did indeed pierce His side, the blood did not pump out, as it would have from a living heart. The blood oozed out as from a heart that had stopped.

Furthermore, we see that blood had obviously collected

and had begun to separate into its constituent parts of red blood corpuscles and white watery serum, because the stains of blood that flowed from the wound had gathered in the middle and spread across the back. Around the edge of them is the clear indication that the blood had divided into its elements. Therefore, there is not a doubt that the man in the Shroud was unquestionably dead.

EVIDENCE FOR THE RESURRECTION

There is also evidence here for the Resurrection. First of all, there is the cause of the image. What created it? Since the team had decided not to look for a supernatural origin to anything, some of the scientists on the team concluded that there is no known possible, natural cause for the image on that shroud. That does leave a supernatural cause. There are those who have speculated that at the moment of His resurrection, Jesus emitted a burst of energy of such a nature that could have produced the scorch on the Shroud, leaving this detailed image.

Furthermore, we see that there was no decomposition in the body, as the Bible says. We also see that the bloodstains, whether they were clots of blood or the thin rivulets of blood that had come down from the wrists and the feet would indubitably be broken or smeared if a shroud were taken off of a body where the blood had dried. This has been proved by repeated tests. We notice that in each of the little rivulets of blood and each of the blood clots there is not the slightest hint, when examined microscopically, of even the edges of these bloodstains being cracked or broken in the slightest way. Which is to say that the scientists have no conception of how that shroud was taken off the body. It could not happen, and yet it did. In short, He appears to have gone right through the cloth.

Lastly, we see that there is a complete correspondence and confirmation of all the biblical details of His suffering, His crucifixion, His burial, and His resurrection. It seems that God has given us another amazing confirmation of His Word. In this day of rampant skepticism, atheism, and unbelief, God seems to be delighting in raising up first one thing and then another to confound the skeptic and the unbeliever to show that His Word is true.

Thank God that He, in His amazing providence, seems to have said, "Save that wrapping for possible future use."

A PLAUSIBLE HISTORY OF THE SHROUD OF TURIN

The Shroud of Turin showed up in 1357 in Lirey, France, in the possession of a family of Crusaders. Prior to that, it had been stolen by French crusaders in the early thirteenth century when they sacked Constantinople. Historian Ian Wilson has made a strong case that the Shroud left Jerusalem in A.D. 30 and traveled up to Edessa in modern-day Turkey. Initially, the Shroud was welcomed by the king (Abgar V), whose contact with it reportedly cured his leprosy. When a later king took over, some 20 years later, about A.D. 57, he rejected the Christian faith and persecuted the followers of it. Some of them hid the cloth in the city walls, where it was not discovered until 525, when workmen were repairing the walls after damage from a flood. They hid it so well that it was hermetically sealed. During this 500-year absence of the Shroud, pictures and images of Jesus Christ were in no way uniform. Christ often appeared beardless and not in any way like we think of Him today, but from 525 to the present, virtually every image of Jesus is the same. Why? Because they are patterned after the Shroud.

Continuing with the Shroud's history, the story is nearly complete. In the tenth century, a Byzantine Army surrounded the small city of Edessa and demanded the holy relic. After a long siege, the Byzantine forces seized their prized quarry and brought the cloth to Constantinople, the capital city, amid great fanfare. Note that within a hundred years of this event, the Muslims completely destroyed the Christian city of Edessa and changed the name of the town to Urfa. They destroyed the some 350 churches of Edessa, including the one that housed the cloth known as the Mandylion (For the first 1200 years of the Shroud's existence, it was known as the Mandylion. It contained an image "not made by human hands." The cloth was folded in such a way that only the *face* was showing.) It is likely the Mandylion/Turin Shroud would have been destroyed had the Byzantines not seized it.

Then in the early 1200s again, crusading Frenchmen robbed the Byzantines of the treasure. During one of the crusades, the "soldiers of the cross" (many coming from France) turned on their fellow Christians and sacked Constantinople. In the melee that followed, the prized cloth was missing. Note that within 250 years, the Muslims destroyed the Christian civilization of Constantinople in 1453 and changed the name to Istanbul. They not only killed thousands upon thousands of Christians, they also destroyed many of their works of art, considered by them to be idolatrous. Again, it is highly possible the Shroud would have been destroyed, had it not been seized by the French Crusaders.

More than a hundred years passed and the cloth showed up *in a crusader's family* in a sleepy village of Lirey, France. We know where it has been since 1357 and it has been under close supervision. It was moved to its present location, Turin, Italy, in the late 1500s. Contrary to some popular misconceptions, the Shroud has only belonged to the Catholic Church since 1983.[22]

SOME SPECIFIC DETAILS ABOUT THE SHROUD

Here are some facts about the Shroud worth bearing in mind. Some of this recaps what we discussed above:

- The human anatomy represented on the Shroud is 100 percent correct. Knowledge about anatomy on the Shroud includes details that weren't known until the twentieth century. In contrast, fourteenth century knowledge of anatomy was quite limited. If the cloth were the work of a

medieval forger, he knew things that weren't known until centuries later.
- The Shroud was photographed for the first time in 1898, and it was discovered to be a photographic negative. Thus, hundreds of years before photography was invented, here was a photographic negative.
- The photographing of the Shroud led to all sorts of scientific experiments. The vast majority of them, virtually all, in fact, argue for its authenticity, except for one highly publicized experiment (the carbon-14 dating of 1988, which critics argue drew from only one sample, a rewoven part of the Shroud). The carbon-14 testing concluded that the Shroud must have been a hoax because it was dated to about 1300 or so. (Of the *thousands* of scientific studies on the Shroud, virtually *all* of which have argued for its authenticity, guess which one the media picked up on?)
- The faint image on the Shroud was not painted on. It was lightly burned on. It is as if at the moment of the Resurrection, Christ's body let off a burst of radiation, as His body changed from mortal to immortal. The image on the Shroud is created by some sort of scorching process. Yet it is only lightly scorched (in a way that didn't destroy the cloth). The image is only .005 of an inch thick. Although there are a few traces of pigment on the Shroud (because as a holy relic, they put paintings in contact with it, presumably to receive a blessing or the like), the image is not comprised of pigment or paint.
- The blood on the Shroud is real human blood. It did not see decay. He was sandwiched inside that cloth for less than 72 hours, yet the blood was undisturbed, which means He somehow went through the cloth; it was not yanked off of Him.
- What you and I think Jesus looked like is based on the Shroud of Turin. People have a universal picture of how they think Jesus looked. Most people do not realize, though, that that image is based on the Shroud of Turin.

The Shroud of Turin

In fact, when the Shroud was hidden away for several centuries—lest it be destroyed by the pagan rulers—pictures of Jesus, as found in the catacombs, varied. (We would not recognize Him as Jesus.) After the Shroud was unearthed in 525 A.D., virtually all pictures of Jesus—icons, coins, etc., began to be patterned after the Shroud. From the sixth century to the present, what we think Jesus looked like is based on the Shroud (and not vice versa).

- Dr. Alan Whanger, retired professor of Duke Medical School, has studied this issue in great depth. He said that while it takes 14 "points of congruence" to prove fingerprints in a court of law, the Shroud and a sixth century icon contain more than 250 points of congruence.
- The Shroud has caused some liberals and unbelievers to convert to Christianity. Earlier in this book, we talked about those Bible scholars who deny the Resurrection; one of those was John A. T. Robinson, a leading clergyman from England who made quite a splash when he wrote the anti-faith book *Honest To God*. (Robert Funk, founder and director of the Jesus Seminar, indirectly honored him by naming his book after the same pattern; Funk's book is called *Honest to Jesus*.) In 1964, when his book came out, Robinson was a leading clergyman of the Church of England, essentially telling the whole world he didn't believe and that it was irrational to believe in Jesus. But, in the last decade of his life, he had a conversion. He became born again. What changed him? The *scientific* evidence for the Resurrection based on the Shroud.
- There is a lot of nonsense surrounding the Shroud—people worshiping it as they worship images and light candles, but to dismiss the Shroud because of that is simply guilt by association. The twentieth and twenty-first century scientific studies on the Shroud stand on their own. The Shroud has been studied more rigorously and put through more scientific tests than any artifact in history.
- While leading evangelicals are often silent about the

Shroud, and I respect that, I still think people should look into it for themselves, because the evidence is there on yet another front, declaring the Easter message: Jesus is risen.

- In the Middle Ages (and even sometimes today), artistic representations of the crucifixion place the nails in the palms. Yet, the Shroud of Turin places the nails in the wrists. It has now been medically proven that nails in the palms would not suffice to hold a crucified man. It was the Shroud that initiated the medical inquiry into this subject in the first place. The remains of a crucified man found in Israel in 1967 show the nails in the wrists as well.
- The image of the Shroud is three-dimensional. When ordinary photos or paintings are studied through a specific NASA space-age machine (a "VP 8 Image Analyzer"), the image always becomes distorted. However, the Shroud has been proven to have three-dimensional properties. It could not have been a painting.
- The theories of skeptics put forward to explain away the Shroud pay indirect homage to its awesome properties. For example, one recent book proposed that no less a genius than Leonardo de Vinci produced the Shroud—and that he had to secretly crucify a man in the process. However, de Vinci lived about a hundred years *after* the Shroud appeared. Leonardo was born in 1452, and, again, we know where the Shroud has been since 1357. So there goes another theory. Everyone that studies the Shroud of Turin agrees that this is a mystery not easily explained away. I find it fascinating that some modern scientists with sophisticated laboratory equipment set out to figure out some ingenious way a medieval forger could have created what would be the greatest forgery of all time (if it were not genuine), using all sorts of elaborate machines and testing data that such an artist didn't have available to him. Then they declared to the world that they have supposedly solved the mystery of the Shroud.

If it is a hoax, this is no ordinary hoax. The greater evidence argues for its authenticity. As some scientists put it, the Shroud is, if you will, a "snapshot of the Resurrection."

At the very moment Christ rose from the dead, something happened—a burst of radiation perhaps—that left a permanent mark on the front and back of the burial cloth that sandwiched the Man of the Shroud who would not stay buried for long. In short, the best theory is that the Shroud of Turin provides scientific evidence for the resurrection of Christ.

FURTHER READING

I said at the start of our discussion that I believe in the resurrection of Jesus Christ, apart from what I learn from the Shroud of Turin. The scientific data I learn about that artifact only adds to my belief in Christ's passing from death to life. Again, if somehow the Shroud were proven beyond all reasonable doubt to be phony, my belief in the Resurrection would continue to stand.

Meanwhile, the more I read about the Shroud—even the absurd theories put forth to explain it away—the more I believe it is genuine, that it sandwiched Jesus after His death, that He walked through it, and that it survived all these centuries to our scientific age in order to provide space age evidence that Jesus Christ rose from the dead.

New books are coming out all the time about the Shroud—this includes many positive books that confirm that it was indeed the burial cloth of Christ. Let me steer the interested reader toward a couple of these. I highly recommend the work of the Whangers. Dr. Alan Whanger has applied both his knowledge of the human body and his passion for photography to his studies on the Shroud. Together, he and his wife Mary have written: *The Shroud of Turin: An Adventure of Discovery* (Franklin, TN: Providence House, 1998).

In addition, I highly recommend a book by an attorney,

Marc Antonacci, *The Resurrection of the Shroud: New Scientific, Medical and Archaeological Evidence* (New York: M. Evans and Company, Inc., 2000). This book conveys the author's grasp of all the complicated scientific disciplines involved. Antonacci says that if a medieval artist put the Shroud together, look what he would have had to accomplish: "Such an artist would have had to have a knowledge of light negativity, light spectrometry, microscopy, radiology, human physiology, pathology, hematology, endocrinology, forensics, and archaeology. In fact, even with all the technology available to us today at the dawn of the twenty-first century, the Shroud's unique characteristics still cannot be duplicated."[23]

Also, the work of sindonologist Ian Wilson on the Shroud has been groundbreaking. His latest book is recommended—*The Blood and the Shroud: New Evidence That the World's Most Sacred Relic Is Real* (New York: Free Press, 1998). Wilson says about the Turin Shroud: "To try to interpret it as the product of some unknown medieval faker seems rather like arguing for the Taj Mahal being a mere geological accident."[24]

Anybody who takes the time to study the details about the Shroud realizes that it is no ordinary artifact. The more we study it, the more confirmed I think is the conclusion: it is the genuine burial cloth of Jesus Christ, and it provides scientific evidence for His resurrection.

Chapter 3

The Discovery of Never Ending Life

"For as in Adam all die, even so in Christ all shall be made alive."

1 Corinthians 15:22

Paul Harvey, my favorite news commentator, tells a wonderful story by a pastor in Boston who was walking down the street one day. He saw a little rag-a-muffin boy carrying an old beat-up cage containing several shivering little nondescript birds. The preacher stopped him and said, "Son, where did you get those birds?"

The boy replied, "I trapped them, sir, out in the field."

The preacher asked, "What are you going to do with them?"

The little boy said, "I'm going to play with them."

"Well," said the preacher, "you are going to get tired of playing with them after a while and then what are you going to do with them?"

The boy said, "I've got a cat at home, and the cat likes birds. I think I'll feed them to the cat."

And then the preacher said to the boy, "Son, how much will you take for those birds?"

The boy answered, "Why, Mister, they are no good. They are

just old field birds. You wouldn't want them. They can't sing, they aren't pretty, they can't do anything."

The preacher said, "Well, I am willing to buy them. How much would you charge?"

The boy thought for a moment and said, "Two dollars." The preacher pulled two dollars out of his pocket and gave it to the amazed boy, who disappeared down an alley. The preacher took the birdcage, opened it, and urged the birds one by one out of the cage, and they flew away. The preacher set the cage down beside the pulpit Easter morning and began to tell what seemed to be an unrelated story—a story about the devil in the Garden of Eden and how he trapped two people and then all of their descendants and put them in a cage. He began to play with them, to make them miserable and Christ said, "What are you going to do with them when you get through playing with them and hurting them? The devil replied, "I'm going to kill them. I'm going to damn them." And Christ said, "How much would you take for them?" The devil said, "All of your sweat and all of your blood," and Jesus paid the price and opened the cage.

Christ delivers us from him who has, through the fear of death, kept the whole world in bondage throughout their whole lives. Have you felt the bondage of the fear of death, perhaps in the night season, perhaps when you are looking down into a grave? It has touched all men in one way or another.

Samuel Johnson was a great intellectual. He gave us the first English dictionary. His house in London was the center of the educated, elite society of that town. All of the authors and poets and other literati gathered together to share in the scintillating conversation in the home of Samuel Johnson.

One day the discussion turned to the subject of death, and he said he didn't want to discuss that, and some witty sophisticate said, "Well, why not?" He said, solemnly, "Because, sir, I might be damned."

He said, "What in the world could you possibly mean by that?"

He said, "I mean that I might be condemned by almighty God to eternal and everlasting punishment. That's what I mean, and

The Discovery of Never-ending Life

I will hear no more on it," and he rose and left the room, in the bondage of the fear of death. The great Thomas Carlyle, said,

> Frightful to all men is Death;
>   from of old named King of Terrors.
> Our little compact home of an Existence,
>   where we dwell complaining,
> Yet as in a home, is passing, in dark agonies,
>   into an Unknown of Separation,
> Foreignness, and unconditioned Possibility.

Yes, for those who have thought about it, it is called the King of Terrors. John Dryden put it well: "Death, in itself is nothing; but we fear to be we know not what, we know not where." Or T. S. Eliot, in his masterpiece, *Murder in the Cathedral,* said: "Not what we call death, but what beyond death is not death, we fear, we fear."

So, if death is the King of Terrors, and life is the greatest possession we have, what can we do about this problem? Well, it's interesting how people have dealt with it. First of all, there are those who have attempted to simply postpone it, to push it back as far as they can. And how are we going to do this? By exercise, of course. We need to get in shape, get fit. The best way to do that is to run, and so we had a book on running by Mr. "Running" himself, Jim Fixx, but that sort of died down a bit when Jim dropped dead running.

Aha, it's not what we do; it's what we eat that is important. Vitamins and minerals and herbs by the scores, by the hundreds. That's the secret. At least that's what a book on life extension told us a couple of decades ago. We could live at least 150 years. Then one of the authors had the temerity to up and die at a reasonably young age, and that hasn't got quite the kick that it once had.

Then, of course, those who are in the know realize the secret is in the water. Why, the discoverer of Florida knew that. Ponce de Leon was looking for the Fountain of Youth, and so have several millions of "snow birds" been looking for the fountain of youth where I live in Florida. I'm afraid that none of them have found it.

There are others that simply try to ignore it. They take the ostrich approach that if they will just stick their head in the sand and say it's not there, they won't have to think about it at all. "Ignorance is bliss" is their motto. Again, interestingly, Sam Johnson said that most men spend all of their time going from one diversion to another simply trying to avoid thinking about their own mortality. Dear friends, what is your current diversion? You cannot get away for too long with that. Eventually, it catches up.

Thirdly, beyond those that postpone or ignore it, there are those that deny that there is anything to it, that dying is really nothing at all, and that is all there is, nothing at all. The late Corliss Lamont, a leading American humanist, said: "I've come to the conclusion that the life which human beings know on this earth is the only one they will ever know. It seems to me we are justified in regarding immortality as an illusion."

Therefore, you have nothing to fear. There's nothing to it. In fact, it may be not the last enemy to be overcome, but a friend to be welcomed, and so, our young people are being taught in school that suicide is a very viable option. It is interesting that we hear a lot about assisted suicide being wrong, and virtually nothing about suicide itself being wrong. If their philosophy is right, and there is nothing after that, what is wrong with suicide? We know that that is not the truth. The old saying applies here too: It is out of the frying pan . . . and, I'm afraid, into the fire.

Thomas Scott was a skeptic and a humanist like Corliss Lamont, with this exception: He had traveled down the humanist road farther. He had reached the edge of the precipice, and he could feel the ground giving way beneath his feet, and he said this: "Until this moment I thought there was neither God nor a Hell; now I know and feel that there are both and I am doomed to perdition by the just judgment of the Almighty." But it was too late . . . too late.

Tragically, millions of our young people are being taught this philosophy of life today in our schools. We have suicide training for children—teaching them various ways of doing it. We even have classes where they teach them how to make their own caskets. Of course, they just shrug it off, because it doesn't really mean anything, does it? Oh, between the ages of 16 and 24, in a recent

The Discovery of Never-ending Life

eight-year period, 39,000 American young people killed themselves (they were well taught in that subject). Tens of thousands more attempted it. No, it is not something that can be ignored, and it cannot be denied. It is very real. After the Columbine tragedy, ABC-TV News did a search of their story archives to see if they had covered that school in any previous segment. They had in 1991—on the subject of Death Education.

I think of an atheist who spent his whole life saying that there was no God, no Heaven, and no Hell. There was nothing. Death was simply the cessation of being. At length, he came to his last day. He was propped up in his bed and his wife was attending him. They were carrying on a conversation, when suddenly he looked beyond her and saw something that was so terrifying to him that his eyes bulged out and his chin fell open. He tried to say something, but could not speak.

His wife screamed and ran out of the room to get help. When she came back, he was still lying there propped against his pillows with his eyes bulging out of his head and his mouth wide open, seeing something so horrific and terrible that he could not even say what it was, but for him, it was too late. That hollow-eyed, lank-jawed skull with the bony beckoning finger had already come for him.

Those who have been wiser than that know that there is something beyond. Shakespeare, considered one of the most brilliant men who ever lived, put it well in the words of Hamlet's soliloquy, part of which says:

> To die: to sleep;
> To sleep: perchance to dream: ay, there's the rub,
> For in that sleep of death what dreams may come,
> When we have shuffled off this mortal coil
> Must give us pause. There's the respect
> That makes calamity of so long life.
>
> But that dread of something after death,
> The undiscover'd country from whose bourn
> No traveller returns, puzzles the will

>And makes us rather bear those ills we have
>Than fly to others that we know not of?
>Thus conscience does make cowards of us all.

Shakespeare himself knew that Jesus Christ is the only true solution to death. Note what the bard said in his will: "I commend my soul into the hands of God my Creator, hoping and assuredly believing through the only merits of Jesus Christ my Saviour, to be made partaker of life everlasting; and my body to the earth, whereof it is made."[25]

There is something to be denied, but it cannot be denied, for it will inevitably make its presence known. There are those who try to distort it, pervert it, but the fact of it is that the Scriptures have said it very well. "And as it is appointed for men to die once, but after this the judgment" (Hebrews 9:27). After the judgment, there is either Heaven, immortality, glory, Paradise forever and ever, or there is the condign punishment for our sins in Hell.

Well, if we cannot deny it, what must we do? We must conquer it. "Conquer death, you say?" Yes. "Well, that is quite a task that you are proposing." Yes, it is. I am happy to say that I have One who is capable of undertaking and accomplishing that task, and that is Jesus Christ, the great hero of God, who came into this world for the very purpose of destroying him who has the power of death and freeing us from the bondage of the fear of death. He was the One who faced death eye-to-eye and conquered death on the first Easter by rising from the dead. That is why Christ is the greatest person who ever lived, because He conquered the greatest problem mankind has.

Did it ever occur to you that there is no Easter in Islam? There is no Easter in Hinduism. There is no Easter in Buddhism. There is no Easter in Judaism. There is no Easter in Jainism, There is no Easter in the religion of Lao-tse or Zoroastrianism. Only in Christianity. And also, there is no Calvary in any of those. Only Christ, the Son of God, came to die and pay the penalty for all of our sins and rise again from the dead to show that God had accepted that and that the portals of Paradise had been opened for all who will place their trust in Him and accept Him as their Savior and Lord. They can be free of the fear of death.

I am happy to say to you that by His great victory I have been set free. Shackles have been broken and I, who once was terrified of death, have no fear of it at all, and I have faced it on several occasions.

Are you still in the bondage of fear? You can be set free. Look unto Jesus. By simply trusting in Him as your atoning sacrifice, as your Savior for sin, as your only hope of Heaven. Abandon all trust in yourself, in your own goodness, your own righteousness, of which you have none, and place your trust in Him, and you will come to *know* that you have eternal life and that you will never really die. Jesus Christ, the Conqueror of Death, said, "I am He who lives, and was dead, and behold, I am alive forevermore" (Revelation 1:18). And because I live, those of you that trust in me shall live also" (John 14:19b).

Have you done that, dear friend? Now is the time to place your trust in Christ, to discover the secret to never-ending life. The secret is in a Cross and an open tomb—the only answer to be found in all of the world.

The ancient pagans had no hope. Life was very dreary. They had no expectation they would rise from the dead. Socrates was, no doubt, one of the most brilliant intellects who ever graced this planet, but at the end of his life, having been condemned by the masters of Athens for perverting the youth, he was given the cup of hemlock, which he drank. As he breathed his last few breaths, and his eyelids began to flutter, his disciples, who had gathered around, leaned close to ask one last question, "Master, shall we live again?"

"I hope so, but no man can know."

WE CAN KNOW

I know. "These things have I written. . . That ye may know that ye have eternal life" (1 John 5:13). "Because I live, ye shall live also" (John 14:19). And Jesus Christ's resurrection is the first fruits of them that slept. That is something every Christian can know. He can know that because Christ suffered and died for his sins and rose again from the dead that he can live with Him forever. Not only that, he need not fear the grave.

When Jesus was born, the angels said, "Fear not." When the angel appeared at the tomb, he said to the women, "Fear not." When Jesus appeared to John, he said, "Fear not." Jesus can take away the fear. He breaks the bands of death, and destroys the power of Satan, who has kept mankind in bondage through fear of death. Again, I, too, have faced death, and I have been 100 percent unafraid—not because I am a hero, but because I trust in the greatest Hero that ever was, in that One who confronted death in His own domain and destroyed the power of Satan.

The angels came down and not only rolled away the stone, but sat upon it as if they were saying, "Death, O Death, O Hell, O Hades, O devil, who will roll this stone back again? Come and try it if you can." Death, the King of Terrors, has been destroyed.

> Who shall rebuild for the tyrant his prison?
> The scepter lies broken that fell from his hands.
> His dominion is ended; our Lord is arisen
> The helpless shall soon be released from their bands.
> No, death has lost its sting.

A father and two boys were out for a picnic in a woods one day. A huge bumblebee came buzzing around and stung one of the boys on the arm. He cried out in pain as he rolled around on the ground. Then the bee began to buzz around the other boy. The father looked at the son who had been stung. The other boy was flailing and screaming and crying and running. The father said to him, "Son, don't run. Don't cry. Don't be afraid. The bee has left his stinger in your brother."

So death has left its sting in our elder brother, Jesus Christ, our Savior from sin. All of that power of death was unleashed upon Him so that we may not have fear.

Just recently, I talked to a couple who visited our church for

The Discovery of Never-ending Life

the first time. The woman told me that she was dead just a few months ago. Her heart had stopped. I asked her if it happened again if she knew where she would go. She didn't know for sure. I asked both her and her husband this question: "Suppose that were to happen again, and you were to stand before God and He were to say to you, 'Why should I let you into my Heaven?'" Ah, dear friend, I would press that question upon every one of you reading this book. Why should God let you into Heaven? (Answer that question right now to yourself.)

They both said, "Well, I have tried to live a good life."

He asked, "I've never done anything really bad. I've never really hurt anyone. I deserve it, don't I?"

I had to tell them the Good News and the bad news. The bad news is no, he doesn't deserve it because he, like myself and everyone else in the world, is a sinner, undeserving the least of God's favor. The commandments of God have been transgressed in thought and word and deed, by omission and commission, ten thousand times ten thousand times. All the world has become guilty in His sight and we are condemned already. God is of purer eyes even to look upon iniquity. So we deserve only Hell.

THE GOOD NEWS

The Good News is that Christ took all of our sins on the Cross, paid for them all, and offers eternal life to those who will abandon all trust in themselves and place their trust in Christ. I said, "Dear friend, though that was once my answer as well, today my answer would be, 'Father, the only reason you should let me into your Heaven is because your Son, Jesus Christ, suffered infinitely upon a Cross and paid my way in. I have no other hope but Him.'" I said, "My friend, the difference between you and me is that you are your savior and Christ is mine. I am no better than you are, but my Savior is better than your savior."

Who is *your* Savior? Whom are you trusting? Do you fear the grave, or have you been able to put off that fear because you have received the free gift of eternal life by trusting in Christ alone, by resting your hopes not in what you have done for God, but in what He has done for you upon a Cross? That is the Good News.

Ah, dear friend, there are some of you reading this book who are very near the precipice of eternity. There are some of you reading this who will descend into your graves before Easter is celebrated again—not necessarily merely the old, but some of the young readers as well. How will it be for you then? The greatest problem of all: the matter of death. The greatest Problem Solver of all: Jesus Christ—the only hope beyond the mortician's bench.

Who is your hope? Who is your savior today? Ah, dear one, repent of your sins and invite Christ to come into your life. Trust Him as Savior and Lord of your life, and the bands of the fear of death will be broken, and you will be set free. You will receive the gift of eternal, everlasting life in Paradise. That is what His resurrection is all about.

If you have never asked Jesus Christ to be your Savior and Lord, I suggest you join me in prayer: "Father, if any readers are still trusting in their own supposed goodness—which is nothing but filthy rags in your sight—O God, help them to see those rags for what they are. May they cast them aside and trust in Thee, that they might be clothed in the perfect white robes of Thy righteousness. May they say in their hearts right now, 'Lord Jesus Christ, come into my life. Take over my life. Be Thou the Lord and Master and Savior of my heart. Grant unto me forgiveness and pardon and cleansing and the gift of eternal life. I am sorry for my sins. I know they sent you to the Cross, but I thank you for coming today to send me to Heaven. In Thy name, Amen.'"

May God bless you in your walk with Jesus Christ, the only one who has conquered the grave forevermore. If you prayed that prayer, I have produced a book for your future growth in Christ. It is called *Beginning Again*. I urge for you to write for your free copy today.[26]

Jesus is risen.

He is risen indeed!

Transcript

Who Is This Jesus: Is He Risen?[27]

This program is made possible by Coral Ridge Media, Inc., the Richard and Helen DeVos Foundation, and the James D. and Millicent C. Massey Foundation.

INTRODUCTION

Person on the Street
Jesus is my "Higher Power."

Francis Martin, John Paul II Institute
Jesus was not a UFO.

Person on the Street
To me, He's God.

Paul L. Maier, Professor of Ancient History at Western Michigan University
Did Jesus rise from the dead?

John Dominic Crossan, Former Co-Chairman, The Jesus Seminar
We don't know for sure.

Person On The Street
Yes, I believe He rose again from the dead. Yeah.
Person On the Street
I do not believe that Jesus Christ rose from the dead.

Josh McDowell, Author of Evidence That Demands A Verdict
It's the most fantastic fact of history.

Narrator
Coral Ridge Media presents an in-depth look at an age-old question: "Who is this Jesus? Is He Risen?"

Dean Jones (Co-host)
This ancient monastery, built in 1141 A.D,[28] was occupied by monks

WHO IS THIS JESUS: IS HE RISEN?

for nearly 700 years. They dedicated themselves to a life of faith in Christ. Now, it has been 2,000 years since Jesus was born, and yet His influence continues to grow through the years, affecting the lives of people from virtually every culture and nation. Hello, I'm Dean Jones. Join me for the next hour as we journey through the claims and counterclaims about this man Jesus. Who was He? Some claim He was just a man . . . others claim He was divine. Why should it matter? We'll hear the opposing views of leading scholars—Protestant, Catholic, Jewish—and hear all sides, be they skeptics or believers. We will attempt to answer the question: Who is this Jesus?

<u>Person on the Street</u>
I know Jesus was a real person

<u>Person on the Street</u>
I'm not the best one for this . . .

<u>Person on the Street</u>
He was here on earth . . .

<u>Person on the Street</u>
I'm not really that religious.

<u>Person on the Street</u>
The Savior of the world . . .

<u>Person on the Street</u>
Character from a book . . .

<u>Person on the Street</u>
But He was a nice guy . . .

<u>Person on the Street</u>
It's all so personal . . .

<u>Person on the Street</u>
I believe that He was the Son of God.

<u>Person on the Street</u>
I believe in Jesus. That's it.

<u>Francis Martin, John Paul II Institute</u>
Jesus Christ has been the most powerful influence in the history of the world.

<u>Richard A. Horsley, University of Massachusetts, Boston</u>
Jesus was a martyr . . .

<u>Helmut Koester, Harvard Divinity School</u>

A prophet and wisdom Teacher . . .

N. T. Wright, Westminster Abbey
A first century Palestinian Jew . . .

Catherine Clark Kroeger, Gordon-Conwell Seminary
Many things . . .

N. T. Wright, Westminster Abbey
The incarnate Son of God . . .

Catherine Clark Kroeger, Gordon-Conwell Seminary
. . . to many people.

John Dominic Crossan, Former Co-Chairman of the Jesus Seminar
Jesus was God walking around in sandals.

INTRODUCTION TO "VARIETY OF OPINIONS" SECTION

Dean Jones
Whatever your view of Him, you must admit that Jesus of Nazareth has impacted life on planet earth as much or more as anyone who ever lived. For this program today, we spoke with scholars from Harvard, Princeton, Notre Dame, Westminster Abbey, and other prestigious institutions and found a wide variety of opinions.

D. A. Carson, Trinity Evangelical Divinity School
Jesus of Nazareth is the very disclosure of God Himself in human form.

John Dominic Crossan, Former Co-Chairman of the Jesus Seminar
He certainly was not in the least bit interested in starting a new religion.

Helmut Koester, Harvard Divinity School
I'm sure that Jesus did not think He was the Messiah.

Sam Lamerson, Knox Theological Seminary
Jesus is God in human flesh.

Narrator
How can the layperson make sense of all the differences of opinions among scholars? On the one hand, there is the traditional position, articulated in the Christian creeds and believed by millions through the centuries, including many scholars today. On the other hand, there are contrasting views often taught in colleges and seminaries and widely presented in the media that challenge many of the foundational beliefs of the Christian Church.

R. C. Sproul, Knox Theological Seminary
There has been a wholesale abandonment of the authority of Scripture.

Narrator
So, scholars debate back and forth on such issues as the reliability of the Gospels. . . .

Richard A. Horsley, University of Massachusetts, Boston
None of the four Gospels are reliable.

N. T. Wright, Westminster Abbey
The Gospels are very reliable.

Paul L. Maier, Professor of Ancient History at Western Michigan University
They are enormously reliable.

John Dominic Crossan, Former Co-Chairman, The Jesus Seminar
I'm not convinced that we have historical accounts.

Narrator
. . . the resurrection of Jesus Christ from the dead . . .

Amy-Jill Levine, Vanderbilt Divinity School
I don't think Jesus' body actually rose from the dead in a physical sense.

N. T. Wright, Westminster Abbey
Since everybody knew that a crucified Messiah was a failed Messiah, the only thing that explains why they said Jesus was Messiah is that they really did believe he had been bodily raised from the dead.

Narrator
. . . and was that spiritual in nature?

John Dominic Crossan, Former Co-chairman of the Jesus Seminar
So, is this some kind of a special vision or . . .what exactly is this?

Narrator
. . . or did Jesus walk out of the tomb?

Gary Habermas, Author of *The Historical Jesus*
The same Jesus who was buried was the Jesus who was raised.

INTRODUCTION TO "THE GOSPELS" SECTION

Dean Jones:
The peacefulness of this chapel, where monks prayed and meditated

Transcript

for hundreds of years, stands in stark contrast to the scholarly controversy now surrounding Christ. One scholar says this, another something else. How do we make sense of it? For this program, we have asked an internationally respected scholar to help us navigate our way through the maze of confusing and conflicting opinions. Dr. D. James Kennedy holds nine advanced degrees, including a Ph.D. in world religion from New York University, and has written over 45 books about New Testament issues. He was selected by the Cambridge Biographical Centre as one of the outstanding intellectuals of the twentieth century. Dr. Kennedy, welcome.

D. James Kennedy
Thank you, Dean.

Dean Jones
With all the varying opinions about Jesus Christ, just how do we sort our way through it all?

D. James Kennedy
Well, imagine a legal trial. Each side brings its own experts with their own interpretation of the facts at hand. How do we finally figure out the truth? By a careful examination of the evidence.

Dean Jones
Evidence is what this program is all about. Some of it is evidence many of us have never seen before. Who is this Jesus? Let's start with the written accounts about Him— the Gospels: Matthew, Mark, Luke, and John. What are they?

Title Graphic: Matthew, Mark, Luke and John

Person on the Street
Theoretically, it's supposed to be . . .

Person on the Street
Matthew, Mark . . .

Person on the Street
The Word of God.

Person on the Street
. . . Luke and John . . .

Person on the Street
Who wrote the Gospels?.

Person on the Street
I can't.

Person on the Street
No.

Person on the Street
Nope.

Person on the Street
Matthew, Mark, Luke, and John

Person on the Street
Those things are two thousand years old.

Person on the Street
Matthew, Mark, Luke, and John.

THE GOSPELS SEGMENT

D. A. Carson, Trinity Evangelical Divinity School
You are talking about things that were described in writing within the living memory of real people who had gone through them. You have four painted portraits, all by different authors, all of the same figure, but from different stances and different light and with a different signature to the author contributing to the richness and the fullness of what this Person is like. That is the kind of testimony we have in the four Gospels.

Amy-Jill Levine, Vanderbilt Divinity School
But does each Gospel somehow get a true handle on Jesus?

Narrator
Dr. Amy-Jill Levine, Jewish Scholar of the New Testament, Vanderbilt Divinity School, doesn't consider Jesus divine, but does assert that the Gospels are substantially reliable.

Amy-Jill Levine, Vanderbilt Divinity School
Yes, each one has some part of what would be considered biographical material.

Narrator
The Gospels were written portraits of the birth, life, death, and resurrection of Jesus Christ and were penned by four disciples that bear their names. Matthew, a former tax collector, was one of the 12 apostles; Mark, a student of both Peter and Paul; Luke, a physician by trade, was also a detailed historian; John, the apostle, wrote three other books in the Bible which bear his name. . .and he wrote the book of Revelation.

D. A. Carson, Trinity Evangelical Divinity School
Do I find such witnesses credible? Absolutely.

Transcript

Narrator
Some scholars have a different view as to why the Gospels were written.

Helmut Koester, Harvard Divinity School
The Gospels were not written in order to preserve the memory of Jesus. The Gospels were written in order to serve as a manual for the Christian churches.

Narrator
Dr. Helmut Koester, Harvard Divinity School

Helmut Koester, Harvard Divinity School
The Gospels are not biographies of Jesus.

Narrator
Traditional scholars have held that these first century authors wrote as eyewitnesses, or from those who wrote what eyewitnesses said.

D. A. Carson, Trinity Evangelical Divinity School
You must not think of the Gospels as videotape recordings.

Narrator
Dr. D. A. Carson, Trinity Evangelical Divinity School,

D. A. Carson, Trinity Evangelical Divinity School
They are, on the other hand, accurate, faithful, selected witness to what happened. They circulated widely, and when they were presented, they were presented with names. It was the Gospel of Jesus Christ according to a particular witness.

Bruce Metzger, Princeton Theological Seminary
Luke tells us at the opening paragraph of his Gospel that he made a thorough search among those who were eyewitnesses.

Reader
Luke 1: "Many have undertaken to draw up an account of the things that have been fulfilled among us, just as they were handed down to us by those who from the first were eyewitnesses and servants of the Word. Therefore, since I myself have carefully investigated everything from the beginning it seemed good also to me to write an orderly account . . . so that you may know the certainty of the things you have been taught" (Luke 1:1-4).

Narrator
Dr. Bruce Metzger, Professor of New Testament Language and Literature, now retired from Princeton Theological Seminary. Many consider him the most universally respected New Testament scholar alive today.

Bruce Metzger, Princeton Theological Seminary
They would seek out the material that originated if they could find out from eyewitnesses, and it's that kind of material that gets put into Matthew, Mark, Luke, and John.

Narrator
Knowing what the Gospels are is one thing, but scholars also seek to answer when they were written. Most place the death of Christ at or around 30 A.D., but how soon after His death were the Gospels written?

Robert Yarbrough, Trinity Evangelical Divinity School
The date of the authorship of the Gospels is a difficult question.

Narrator
Professor at Trinity Evangelical Divinity School, Dr. Robert Yarbrough

Robert Yarbrough, Trinity Evangelical Divinity School
I would be willing to put the earliest Gospel any time after around 40 A.D., and the latest Gospel anytime as late as, perhaps, the nineties A.D.

D. A. Carson, Trinity Evangelical Divinity School
There is a great deal of contemporary thought that tries to late date all the Gospels and argues that none of the canonical Gospels was written until after A.D. 70. I don't agree with that. Historically, most Christian scholars have not agreed with it.

Narrator
Why is the date of the Gospels significant? Because some modern scholars think the later that they were written, the less accurate they are. Dr. Helmut Koester, Harvard Divinity School:

Helmut Koester, Harvard Divinity School
None of the Gospels is written before the year 70; that is forty years after the death of Jesus. All the disciples were most likely dead at that time, so it's not personal memory that goes from Jesus' preaching and ministry to the Gospels . . .

Narrator
What causes Dr. Koester and others to hold this opinion? First, it helps to understand the background. Matthew, Mark and Luke[29] all record that in the last week of Jesus' life, He sat on the Mount of Olives, looked into the city and predicted that Jerusalem and its temple would be destroyed within one generation. Jerusalem was, in fact, leveled by Rome in 70 A.D., and here is where scholars are divided: Many modern scholars who don't believe in miracles, like predictive prophecy, would

Transcript

assume that the Gospel writers are putting words in Jesus' mouth after the fact.

Helmut Koester, Harvard Divinity School
We know that Jesus was most likely a prophet and a wisdom teacher, but not someone who was predicting the future.

Narrator
Therefore, in the opinion of scholars like Dr. Koester, Gospel writers like Mark are, in fact, reflecting a memory.

Helmut Koester, Harvard Divinity School
Mark reflects the Jewish war from 66 to 70 A.D. There is clear memory that the Jewish war had happened and that Jerusalem was destroyed

Paul L. Maier, Professor of Ancient History at Western Michigan University
Many liberal scholars suggest that the Gospels were written after the destruction of Jerusalem. Why? Because Jesus makes such an accurate prediction on the way to the Cross that indeed, Jerusalem would be destroyed. That is called prophecy after the fact, shall we say.

Narrator
So, it goes back to the underlying assumption, discounting miracles like predictive prophecy. But traditional scholars point out that there is scriptural evidence which leads us to believe that Matthew, Mark and Luke were written before the fall of Jerusalem, and one such example involves the Gospel of Matthew.

Paul L. Maier, Professor of Ancient History at Western Michigan University
Now Matthew, as you know, delights in prophecy/fulfillment, prophecy fulfillment—those couplets. So often Matthew says, "This was accomplished by Jesus that it might be fulfilled what the prophet said," and so on. Can you imagine that if the book of Matthew had been written after the fall of Jerusalem, wild horses couldn't have prevented Matthew from saying, "And Jesus' prediction was fulfilled when Jerusalem was destroyed." He doesn't say that, and that's very unlike Matthew.

Narrator
So, most traditional scholars believe Matthew was written before 70 A.D. The same holds true for the dating of the Gospels of Mark and Luke.[30]

Paul L. Maier, Professor of Ancient History at Western Michigan University

The arguments that these sources were written many years after the events they report are not true.

INTRODUCTION TO "GOSPEL RELIABILITY" SECTION

<u>Dean Jones</u>
Now, despite disagreement among scholars as to exactly when the Gospels were written, the real issue is: Are they reliable? Right?

<u>D. James Kennedy</u>
Absolutely, Dean, and how you answer that question often depends on your starting point. For example, the life of Christ is filled with miracles. But, if a scholar, or a layman, for that matter, assumes that miracles, or the supernatural, are impossible, he is going to conclude that each individual miracle, in its turn, is also impossible.

<u>Dean Jones</u>
So it's not just the information that counts, it's the assumptions by which we interpret that information.

<u>D. James Kennedy</u>
Precisely.

<u>Dean Jones</u>
All right, let's hear from the experts, now, on a crucial issue: Are the Gospels reliable?

Title Graphic: The Gospel Truth?

<u>Person on the Street</u>
Reliable? Yes.

<u>Person on the Street</u>
No.

<u>Person on the Street</u>
You don't think they are reliable?

<u>Person on the Street</u>
To a reasonable degree they are.

<u>Person on the Street</u>
It's a nice book. . . .

<u>Person on the Street</u>
You're going by hearsay situation.

Transcript

Person on the Street
... inspired by God.

GOSPEL RELIABILITY

N. T. Wright, Westminster Abbey
The Gospels are very reliable accounts of what was going on in Jesus' life, and particularly His death, around 30 A.D.

Richard Horsley, University of Massachusetts, Boston
We can't ever expect that we get right back to an accurate report of exactly what Jesus did or said.

Narrator
These are two assertions over which scholars debate. Are the Gospels reliable?

Richard A. Horsley, University of Massachusetts, Boston
We would say the Gospels aren't reliable as accurate historical accounts because that's not what they set out to do.

Narrator
For some scholars, such as Dr. Richard Horsley, head of the Religion Department of the University of Massachusetts, Boston, the position of Gospel reliability is simply not defendable because the four Gospels were designed to promote a social or political agenda.

Richard A. Horsley, University of Massachusetts, Boston
In proclaiming the Kingdom of God, saying, "Well, God is already taking care of the political revolution; now we can carry out the social revolution here in our villages. Now we can," repeating the sayings of Jesus, "love our enemies, do good, lend to our neighbors, and restore these village communities."

Narrator
But traditional scholars assert the Gospels aren't primarily social or political but, in fact, religious in nature. They assert that what we have in the Gospels is what actually took place. These four Gospels include the disciple's foibles, mistakes, and failures—evidence of the authors' concern for accuracy.

N. T. Wright, Westminster Abbey
The disciples in the Gospels are a very mixed bunch. These people went on to be the leaders of the Church. It would have been very easy for the early Church to write up the stories in such a way that you always have the disciples exactly understanding everything and saying, "Yes,

Master, of course," and at once going off and doing it. Instead, you have them as a completely muddled bunch that have clearly their own agendas of what they thought Jesus was about. They are more and more puzzled because there is a mismatch between what they think Jesus is supposed to be doing. Actually, that, too, is part of the historical reliability of the tradition.

Narrator
Another argument is that the Gospels are simply myths. Dr. John Dominic Crossan, former co-chairman of the Jesus Seminar:

John Dominic Crossan, Former Co-chairman of the Jesus Seminar
If you were to say, for example, that the Greco-Roman claims were myths and were legends, but when you come to the stories of Christianity, these were facts, I would say that is simply untrue for the first century.

Narrator
Noted scholar and author C. S. Lewis would disagree. Lewis spent a lifetime studying texts. As a professor of medieval and Renaissance literature at both Oxford and Cambridge, he was well versed in textual criticism, and he argued it is not so simple to say the Gospels are myths. They don't sound like myths and calling them myths leads to a logical contradiction. In his book, *Between Heaven and Hell*, Dr. Peter Kreeft, Professor of Philosophy at Boston College, sums up Professor Lewis' argument: "If the Gospels are not eyewitness accounts, then they are a type of fantasy that has absolutely no parallel in all of literature. That some Galilean peasants—fishermen and tax collectors—invented not only the world's most gigantic and successful hoax, but a totally unique form of literature, the 'realistic fantasy.'" So traditional scholars assert that the Gospels are not politics and not myths. The word "gospel" in Greek means "good news" and that is what they are intended to be—a positive proclamation based on true events.

Josh McDowell, Author of *Evidence That Demands A Verdict*
I believe there is more evidence for the historical reliability of the New Testament than any ten pieces of classical literature combined.

Narrator
Noted author Josh McDowell has written or co-authored some 70 books on various faith related subjects.

Josh McDowell, Author of *Evidence That Demands A Verdict*
Matthew and John wrote as eyewitnesses. "What our eyes have seen, our ears have heard, our hands have handled we declare unto you." They said, "We were witnesses of the miracles and everything of Jesus Christ." They wrote as eyewitnesses. Or like Luke. Luke was not an eye-

witness. Luke said, "I have taken everything and examined it carefully from those who were eyewitnesses."

Narrator
At the time the Gospels were being written, there was fierce opposition to the fledgling Christian Church. If any document, like Mark or Luke, appeared <u>falsely</u> claiming to be filled with eyewitness material, those opposed would immediately have exposed the lie.

Josh McDowell, Author of *Evidence That Demands A Verdict*
The presence of hostile and antagonistic witnesses actually became one of the most powerful forces to determine truth. They didn't dare to fabricate.

Narrator
This hostility not only confirms the Gospels' claim to contain eyewitness testimony; it further insured that the authors remained reliable on *every* other point, including the miracles of Jesus.

Josh McDowell, Author of *Evidence That Demands A Verdict*
There were people there that hated what the disciples stood for, hated what the apostles stood for, and immediately, they would have nailed them. They would have corrected them and said, "Wait a minute. I was there. Jesus didn't say that. Jesus didn't do that. He didn't go there."

Narrator
Yet eyewitness material alone does not make something reliable. Let's look at other evidence that supports the claim that the Gospels are reliable. There is the question of the motive and the character of the writers.

Francis Martin, John Paul II Institute
There is the simple question of the honesty of the men who wrote these texts. Why would they lie? What would they gain from it? Most of them, it cost their lives to preach this.

Narrator
Father Francis Martin, John Paul II Institute, further suggests that the kinds of stories told in the Gospels are yet more evidence of reliability.

Francis Martin, John Paul II Institute
Another dimension of reliability is that if I am starting a world movement, I would hardly tell all these embarrassing stories about myself—how I failed to believe Jesus, how I betrayed him, how I denied him. The Gospels are full of these things, particularly the Gospel of Mark, who takes the great leaders of the Church and uses them as examples of what not to do.

Sam Lamerson, Knox Theological Seminary
I believe that the New Testament documents are reliable.

Narrator
Dr. Sam Lamerson, Knox Theological Seminary

Sam Lamerson, Knox Theological Seminary
We ask ourselves, "What in those documents seems to be truthful and seems to be the sort of thing a person wouldn't have made up, and there are a variety of things like that.

Narrator
This argument is that the Gospels have an aura of authenticity, which comes to light when we understand the cultural background.

Sam Lamerson, Knox Theological Seminary
For instance, the women being the first ones who show up at the tomb. Women were not, in that day and age, looked upon very highly. All one has to do is read first century Jewish documents, and you realize they couldn't give testimony in a court of law; they couldn't report about what they had seen, and so if somebody is making up a story, certainly they're not going to have the women be the ones who show up first.

Narrator
So, the argument goes, if they were making all this up, they would have chosen examples that their culture would have trusted—not women . . . or shepherds.

Sam Lamerson, Knox Theological Seminary
In first century Judaism, the shepherds were one of the lowest of occupations. They were looked upon as dishonest; they also couldn't give testimony in the court of law. And yet the first appearance of Jesus, in the Gospel of Luke, is to the shepherds. That is not something someone is going to make up.

Paul L. Maier, Professor of Ancient History at Western Michigan University
What is clear is that we cannot footnote every verse in the Gospels from secular sources. There are some aspects of the nativity account that we can't get at. For example, there is no way to use these outside disciplines—history, archaeology, geography—to guarantee that the angel Gabriel appeared to Mary.

Narrator
While the Gospels contain elements we cannot verify, they certainly contain many elements that withstand modern methods of historical scrutiny.

Transcript

Paul L. Maier, Professor of Ancient History at Western Michigan University
Every time there is a base on which we can build a bridge, some reference to a political figure, a reference to a place, a reference to an episode, that is the sort of thing we can check up on to see if the Scriptural record is accurate or not. Time and again we can build bridges all over the place. There are many, many different points of tangency. For example, the Gospel according to St. Luke loves to build bridges out into the secular evidence. How does the nativity account begin? He begins with the great Augustus. Everyone knew who Augustus was—the virtual founder of the Roman Empire. This is Luke's way of saying that these things were not done in a corner somewhere.

Narrator
Dr. Paul Maier, Professor of Ancient History at Western Michigan University, Kalamazoo

Paul L. Maier, Professor of Ancient History at Western Michigan University
But what is so interesting is that if you try to compare the Gospel accounts against their context in the ancient world—if you check out, for example, even the geographical references in the Gospel—are they accurate or are they not? Are these place names—place names of villages, towns, cities, provinces, mountains, valleys, rivers, seas—accurate or not? And the fact is, they are . . . they are. They're 100 percent identifiable today in so many cases.

Francis Martin, John Paul II Institute
The Gospels are reliable. We can rely on them to mediate to us a deep understanding of Jesus Christ, who walked on this earth. But you have to remember that the Gospels are not written to promote or defend the memory of a dead master. They are written to put us in touch with the living Lord.

INTRODUCTION TO "JESUS SEMINAR" SECTION

Dean Jones
Dr. Kennedy, this issue of reliability is clearly a contested one.

D. James Kennedy
It certainly is, Dean, and one group that certainly believes that the Gospels are NOT reliable is called the Jesus Seminar.

Dean Jones
I've heard of them.

D. James Kennedy
That's because when the press needs a quote about Christ, they quite frequently will call on members of the so-called Jesus Seminar. Now they believe that only 18 percent of the words of Christ, as seen in the Gospels, were actually spoken by Jesus for sure.

Dean Jones
They feel only 18 percent were actually His words? If that is true and they receive so much press, well, maybe we should know a little bit more about them.

D. James Kennedy
I certainly agree.

Dean Jones
All right, let's take a closer look now at the Jesus Seminar.

Title Graphic: Who Speaks for the Scholars?

Person on the Street
My experience with college professors is that they have more of an agenda.

Person on the Street
They want to see what their opinion is on it.

Person on the Street
Of course, I believe that they believe what they are saying.

Person on the Street
I mean, I listen to everybody objectively.

Person on the Street
Whatever they say makes no difference to me.

Person on the Street
I more tend to believe someone who has studied it for his or her life.

Person on the Street
No, I believe whatever I believe myself.

Transcript

Narrator
For some, one of the most controversial movements in Bible scholarship today is the Jesus Seminar, a group of about 70 scholars. They question the authenticity of many of Jesus' sayings. For example, they believe that in the Lord's Prayer, only the words "Our Father" were genuinely from Jesus. They also question many of His miracles.

John Dominic Crossan, Former Co-chairman of the Jesus Seminar
Could Jesus walk on water? I don't care—whatever. To be quite frank with you, I put it in the same category as UFOs.

Narrator
Dr. John Dominic Crossan, former co-chairman of the Jesus Seminar:

John Dominic Crossan, Former Co-chairman of the Jesus Seminar
They meet twice a year for four days and have been doing it since '85 to discuss, to prepare papers, to argue, and then to vote, to come to a conclusion on, for example, a statement like "Blessed are the poor." Do we as a group agree that Jesus "most likely," "likely," "unlikely," or "very unlikely" said that statement.

Richard A. Horsley, University of Massachusetts, Boston
The whole premise of the Jesus Seminar was that we should work on the basis of isolated individual sayings. Now, this strikes me as indefensible as an historical method because any saying depends upon a meaning context.

Francis Martin, John Paul II Institute
They have been able to attract media attention. A part of it is because, as you know, the media looks for what is new, different, exciting, and challenging—particularly to religion.

Narrator
Father Francis Martin is a New Testament scholar at the John Paul II Institute in Washington, D.C. He has spent a lifetime in serious scholarship, studying and publishing all over the world.

Francis Martin, John Paul II Institute
In my opinion, having worked in this field now for about 40 years, 85 percent or more of the scholars in the United States and in Europe would not accept the basic principles of the Jesus Seminar.

Narrator
Father Martin is one of many scholars with serious disagreements with the Jesus Seminar.

Helmut Koester, Harvard Divinity School
The Jesus Seminar certainly does not represent mainstream. I was, in fact, in the first meeting of the Jesus Seminar, and I decided that I didn't want to have anything to do with it.

Narrator
We asked Dr. Robert Funk, the founder and director of the Jesus Seminar for an interview for this program. He declined. Meanwhile, scholars from a wide variety of perspectives do not agree with the basic premises of the Jesus Seminar.

Amy-Jill Levine, Vanderbilt Divinity School
What I find problematic about them is that they frequently leave out the very Jewish things about Jesus. I think Jesus is a very internally focused Jewish man, interested in Jewish law, interested in preparing the Jewish people for God's reign.

Narrator
The vast majority of the members of the Jesus Seminar are academics, not pastors, priests, or rabbis who are accountable to their own congregations.

Jerome Neyrey, University of Notre Dame
I think it's easy to be skeptical like that when one doesn't have any sort of pastoral accountability.

Narrator
Father Jerome Neyrey, Roman Catholic Priest, Professor of Theology at the University of Notre Dame.

Jerome Neyrey, University of Notre Dame
And I think living inside a worshiping, believing community both nourishes what I do with the Scriptures, but it also holds me accountable.

Narrator
Dr. Crossan defends the Jesus Seminars conclusions, especially as they relate to the opinion of the average layperson.

John Dominic Crossan, Former Co-chairman of the Jesus Seminar
If you can't trust scholars, well, quite frankly, you have nothing. Where do you think the Greek New Testament comes from? That comes from a group of scholars. So if you don't like scholars, be very careful.

Narrator
But many scholars themselves take issue with the idea that the Jesus Seminar scholars speak for all Bible scholars.

Transcript

Paul L. Maier, Professor of Ancient History at Western Michigan University
They've tried to co-opt that term for themselves. This, of course, is an insult to what I would call the more serious scholars across the world.

Narrator
Because of his unorthodox views of the Gospels, Dr. Crossan sometimes gets called an atheist. He takes exception to the charge.

John Dominic Crossan, Former Co-chairman of the Jesus Seminar
In the '90s alone I have written a million words about Jesus. If somebody at the end of that calls me an atheist, I have only two conclusions: That person is either—I'll be very blunt—a fool or a liar.

Narrator
Meanwhile, conservative critics of the Jesus Seminar, in general, point out that its overall skeptical conclusions simply reflect the skeptical make-up of most of its participants.

D. A. Carson, Trinity Evangelical Divinity School
The conclusions are no better than the opinions of that particular group.[31]

INTRODUCTION TO "NEW TESTAMENT RELIABILITY" SECTION

Dean Jones
It's hard to believe theologians would argue with so many of the words of Jesus.

D. James Kennedy
Dean, it is absolutely astonishing that they would. But keep in mind that we have been talking about the Jesus Seminar, and they represent a very small portion of New Testament scholarship and, at that, a fringe group.

Dean Jones
All right, let me ask you this: When New Testament scholars are examining the New Testament, what exactly are they working with?

D. James Kennedy
They are working with manuscripts that are, of course, handwritten copies of the original Greek text.

Dean Jones
And how reliable are they?

D. James Kennedy
Well, amazingly, Dean, there is a tremendous amount of agreement among scholars—at least on this point.

Dean Jones
All right, ladies and gentlemen, let's look at some of the evidence concerning the dependability of the New Testament documents.

Title Graphic: A League of Its Own

Person on the Street
Well, I believe in the Ten Commandments.

Person on the Street
I believe it's factual.

Person on the Street
I don't think it should be taken literally.

Person on the Street
It's the translation you have to look at.

Person on the Street
There is a lot of symbolism in the Bible.

Person on the Street
It's the word of man as he sees God.

Person on the Street
It's the most important book in the world.

NEW TESTAMENT DOCUMENTS

Narrator
Matthew, Mark, Luke, and John wrote their accounts nearly 2,000 years ago. Is what we have in today's Bible what they wrote? The printing press wasn't invented until 1456. Until then, monks copied each biblical manuscript by hand, just as had been done for thousands of years before by Jewish scribes. In fact, that is the way the Torah is still copied today. Dr. Paul Maier, Professor of Ancient History.

Paul L. Maier, Professor of Ancient History at Western Michigan University
There was a rule in recopying the Old Testament, for example, that if you made a mistake in the two-page segment, you begin all over again.

Narrator
And fairly recent discoveries have helped confirm the accuracy of

Transcript

this tradition. In 1947, in what is now Israel, near the community of Qumran, a shepherd found scrolls that we have come to call the Dead Sea Scrolls. This find included copies of the Old Testament book of Isaiah. Previous to this find, our earliest known copy of Isaiah was dated tenth century A.D. If we compare, say, Chapter 53 from one of the Dead Sea Scrolls with the tenth century scroll, we discover—after more than 850 years of copying and recopying—virtually no differences, and certainly nothing that changes the meaning.

Paul L. Maier, Professor of Ancient History at Western Michigan University
Showing you, again, the care with which the biblical scribes would transmit this data, and the care that the monks devoted.

Narrator
And similar care has been shown to the transmission of the New Testament text.

Herbert Samworth, The Scriptorium
These copies are written with much care.

Narrator
Dr. Herbert Samworth, director of the Scriptorium, a museum housed in Orlando, Florida,[32] dedicated to how we got our Bible.

Herbert Samworth, The Scriptorium
The monks who copied the Scriptures were very careful because they knew they were dealing with the Word of God.

Amy-Jill Levine, Vanderbilt Divinity School
One can look at the manuscripts of the New Testament positively or negatively. Of the over 15,000 scraps and full manuscripts we have prior to Gutenberg, one can find distinctions, contradictions, different words in pretty much every single one of them.

Narrator
But the key point of this is that in the vast majority of the texts, these minor differences don't change the meaning, nor do they call in dispute any major doctrine.

D. A. Carson, Trinity Evangelical Divinity School
Almost all text critics will acknowledge that 96—even 97 percent— of the text of the Greek New Testament is morally certain; it's just not in dispute.

Narrator
Furthermore, there are more than 5,000 whole or partial copies of

the Greek New Testament. Scholars translate our modern English Bibles from these Greek New Testament texts. There are also thousands of early manuscript copies in other languages, such as Latin, Syriac, Coptic, Armenian, and so on, that are all based on the original Greek manuscripts. Because of the sheer number of the ancient manuscripts, the New Testament is unequaled among the writings of antiquity.

Bruce Metzger, Princeton Theological Seminary
The very fact that there are so many copies still available from ancient times means that the degree of reliability of what has been transmitted to us in the New Testament is at a high level.

Narrator
Now compare the Greek New Testament with other writings of antiquity. Julius Caesar wrote *Gallic Wars*; we have ten known manuscript copies. Plato's *Tetralogies*? There are seven known manuscript copies in existence. The New Testament, however, is in a league of its own with more than 5,000 manuscript copies in the original Greek alone.

Narrator
Outside the Bible, the best attested writings of antiquity are the writings of the Greek author Homer, with 647 total manuscripts in existence. Dr. N. T. Wright serves as the Canon Theologian of Westminster Abbey.

N. T. Wright, Westminster Abbey
The New Testament documents are very reliable. We have better manuscript evidence for the New Testament than for any other ancient book.

Narrator
Furthermore, when one compares the time span between the authors' date of completion and the earliest known manuscript in existence, the historical support for the New Testament is overwhelming. Caesar wrote his *Gallic Wars* some time before his death in 44 B.C., yet the earliest copy in existence is dated 900 A.D.—that is a gap of one thousand years. Plato wrote his *Tetralogies* some time before 347 B.C., yet the earliest manuscript copy is dated around 900 A.D., a time gap of 1,200 years. Contrast this to the New Testament . . . which was completed no later than one hundred A.D., but the earliest known manuscript containing most of the New Testament is dated about 350 A.D. This means that the time gap for the New Testament is only about 250 years, and there are manuscript fragments even earlier than that.

Sam Lamerson, Knox Theological Seminary
It seems to me that if you throw out the reliability of the New Testament

Transcript

documents, one must become an historical agnostic. If you are not going to accept that as basically historically reliable, you cannot accept any writings as historically reliable, because we do not have of them the same amount of backing that we do for the New Testament.

N. T. Wright, Westminster Abbey
The New Testament is simply on a different scale entirely in terms of the depth and range of the manuscript evidence.

INTRODUCTION TO SECTION ON "ANCIENT SOURCES OUTSIDE THE NEW TESTAMENT"

Dean Jones
You know, understanding how we got the Bible makes me appreciate the men who preserved these texts, probably in monasteries like this.

D. James Kennedy
Absolutely, and the fact, Dean, that we have so many manuscripts puts the Bible in a league all of its own among ancient works.

Dean Jones
Now let me ask you this: "Suppose these manuscripts didn't exist. Then what? What could we know, if anything, about Jesus Christ?"

D. James Kennedy
Well, that is an excellent question, Dean, and the fact is, it has been answered quite convincingly.

Title Graphic: Other Voices

Person on the Street
I have never heard of any sources outside the Bible and the New Testament regarding God or Jesus.

Person on the Street
We read about Him in the Koran, right?

Person on the Street
I don't know.

Person on the Street
Josephus tells us a good bit.

Person on the Street
I haven't heard of any other reference about Jesus other than the Bible.

CORROBORATING TEXTS

Narrator
Everything we have seen so far reflects the scriptural evidence regarding Jesus—can we learn anything about Jesus Christ apart from what is in the Bible?

John Dominic Crossan, Former Co-Chairman, The Jesus Seminar
Well, we do know that Jesus existed from both Tacitus, at the beginning of the second century, a pagan historian, and Josephus at the end of the first century.

Narrator
In fact, within the first 150 years of the Christian era, there are several non-Christian writers who mention Jesus and the phenomenal growth of the early Church. Dr. Gary Habermas, author of *The Historical Jesus*.

Gary Habermas, Author of *The Historical Jesus*
Actually, the life of Jesus is recorded in whole or in part, different segments, in about 20 different non-Christian sources, archaeological or historical, outside the New Testament. Now, most of these are little snippets—a sentence here, a paragraph there— but you put them all together and there are approximately 60 to 65 facts concerning the life, death, resurrection, teachings of Jesus in the earliest Church. You can get an outline of His life and never touch the New Testament.

Paul L. Maier, Professor of Ancient History at Western Michigan University
By far the greatest source of extra-biblical (that is non-biblical), knowledge that we can glean from the ancient world comes in the writings of the first century Jewish historian Flavius Josephus.

Narrator
Josephus wrote two historical volumes. A passage from one has had scholars arguing for centuries. Nonetheless, scholars today can reasonably reconstruct what Josephus originally wrote:

Paul L. Maier, Professor of Ancient History at Western Michigan University
"At this time there was a wise man called Jesus, and his conduct was good, and he was known to be virtuous . . . Pilate condemned him to be crucified and to die. But those who had become His disciples did not abandon His discipleship. They reported that He had appeared to them three days after His crucifixion and that He was alive."

Transcript

Narrator
Other examples: two writers who lived in the first century, Thallus and Phlegon, both of whom, independently of each other, made reference to the darkness at noon which occurred when Christ died . . . And there are others.

Paul L. Maier, Professor of Ancient History at Western Michigan University
Suetonius, another Roman historian, talks about punishment inflicted on the Christians.

Narrator
Another source? Pliny the Younger,

Edwin Yamauchi, Professor of Ancient History at Miami University, Ohio
In a celebrated letter that he wrote to his friend, the Emperor Trajan, he speaks about Christians multiplying in his province, and that he has arrested some of them.

Narrator
Dr. Edwin Yamauchi, Miami University, Ohio.

Edwin Yamauchi, Professor of Ancient History at Miami University, Ohio.
They confess that they met before dawn to swear to keep the Ten Commandments, and that they worshipped Jesus as God, and they sang hymns to Him.

Narrator
So we see there are many non-Christian references to Jesus from the first and early second centuries, and if we consider Christian sources, including the Greek and Latin Church Fathers, we find even more evidence.

Bruce Metzger, Princeton Theological Seminary
There are really so many quotations in these patristic writings that if we didn't have any Greek manuscripts, if we didn't have any translations into these other languages, we could reconstruct practically the entire New Testament from the quotations made by the Church fathers.

INTRODUCTION TO "ARCHAEOLOGY" SECTION

Dean Jones
So apart from the book—the Bible—there is still strong evidence for

the life of Christ. Now, is there anything else that backs up the reliability of the New Testament?

D. James Kennedy
Indeed there is, Dean. In fact, archaeology itself amazingly confirms the biblical record.

Title Graphic: Digging Deeper

Person on the Street
Well, archaeology is . . .

Person on the Street
the finding of lost treasure . . .

Person on the Street
. . . kind of boring.

Person on the Street
Those shows about archaeology on TV are pretty cool.

Person on the Street
I know nothing about it.

Person on the Street
Archaeology validates the Bible.

ARCHAEOLOGY

John Dominic Crossan, Former Co-Chairman, The Jesus Seminar
Archaeology neither confirms nor denies the Bible's most important message, which is a challenge to faith.

Richard A. Horsley, University of Massachusetts, Boston
On balance, I think that archaeology has tended to demonstrate that the Bible is reliable, rather than undermine the Bible's reliability.

Narrator
Take a walk through Israel today and you will see many sites claiming to be authentic to the life of Christ. Some may be . . . some not. Is this the actual tomb of Jesus? There is no direct evidence to prove it, and claims like this tend to minimize many of the real contributions of archaeology.

Paul L. Maier, Professor of Ancient History at Western Michigan University
The archaeological evidence correlates beautifully with the Gospel records. You are going to find slight differences from time to time, but

time and again we find that "the stones cry out" very favorably in terms of supporting the biblical record.

Narrator
Before archaeology, critics came up with all sorts of unsubstantiated theories questioning the Bible's accuracy. Then around the year 1900, with the development of the science of archaeology, those critics were silenced . . .

Paul L. Maier, Professor of Ancient History at Western Michigan University
There is no question but that archaeology is the Bible's best friend.

Narrator
But for some, the doubts remain. For example, the Gospel of Luke tells us that Joseph and Mary traveled to Bethlehem at the time of Christ's birth because of a Roman census, but recently some critics have doubted that this census ever took place.

Paul L. Maier, Professor of Ancient History at Western Michigan University
When Augustus died, he had two bronze plaques erected in front of his mausoleum in Rome in which he listed the 36 things for which he most wanted to be remembered. Point number eight: "I took a census of the Empire three times."

Narrator
The Gospels are filled with archaeologically verifiable details. They tell us, for example, Pontius Pilate was the Roman Governor responsible for the crucifixion of Christ. And in the port city of Caesarea, a stone recently uncovered reads, "Tiberium Pontius Pilate, Prefect of Judea."

Sam Lamerson, Knox Theological Seminary
All of a sudden, people are saying, "Oh well, then I guess Pontius Pilate must really have lived." The question, of course, we have to ask is, "Why are you willing to trust a stone, but you're not willing to trust the New Testament?"

Narrator
In Jerusalem there are many traditional sites related to the life of Christ, such as the pool of Siloam, where the Gospel of John reports Jesus cured a paralyzed man; the Garden of Gethsemane, where Christ prayed just before His arrest; the Via Dolorosa, the way of sorrows, where Christ carried His Cross. But apart from these well-known sites, there are many first-century tombs similar to the one mentioned in the Gospels—with large stone

doors. Here is another example: The Scriptures state that before His execution, Jesus appeared before the high priest—whose name was Caiaphas.

Edwin Yamauchi, Professor of Ancient History at Miami University, Ohio
Just recently, in the 1990s, we have discovered an ossuary with the name of Caiaphas. Ossuaries are limestone boxes in which the Jews re-deposited bones of the dead after about a year, when the flesh had rotted away.

Narrator
And the archaeologists keep digging.

N. T. Wright, Westminster Abbey
Archaeology sheds a flood of light on the New Testament, and the more that light shines on the New Testament, the more we say, "Yeah, this makes sense; this fits in its historical context."

INTRODUCTION TO "MESSIANIC PROPHECIES" SECTION

Dean Jones
You know, having been to Israel and seeing some of the rich archaeological digs over there, it's really exciting to see the evidence pointing to the person of Jesus.

D. James Kennedy
It really is, Dean, and another area of evidence for Christ is the hundreds of prophesies from the Old Testament that have been fulfilled by Christ.

Dean Jones
Now wait just a minute. Prophecies? A lot of people when they think of prophecies think of the grocery store and the tabloids and the outlandish predictions of the future. Some would say these are prophecies too. Right?

D. James Kennedy
They are, but the difference between those prophecies and the prophecies of the Bible is very plain. Those in the tabloids are almost always wrong, and those in the Bible are 100 percent right. That is the difference.

Dean Jones
Well, let's see how right they are.

Transcript

Title Graphic: "Is Jesus the Christ?"

Person on the Street
Ah, a prophecy is . . .

Person on the Street
If you look back . . .

Person on the Street
. . . the forecast of an event . . .

Person on the Street
. . . things have come to pass . . .

Person on the Street
. . . that is to take place . . .

Person on the Street
. . . prophecies come true . . .

Person on the Street
. . . that's in the future.

Person on the Street
I think some people do have the gift to see into the future.

MESSIANIC PROPHECIES

Narrator
In the Old Testament, God promised to send His people a Messiah, a Deliverer, a King. In fact, there are over 300 of these kinds of promises—known as Messianic Prophecies—some written over a thousand years before Christ. The question here is: Did Jesus fulfill any of these prophecies? The Hebrew word "Messiah" means "Anointed One," and in Greek, Messiah is "Christ." But not all scholars think Jesus was the Christ.

Helmut Koester, Harvard Divinity School
Just as much as my last name is Koester, so Paul used Christ as the last name of Jesus. Paul thought that Jesus was the Lord and the Son of God. That is very clear, but Paul never speaks of Jesus as the Messiah.

Narrator
And yet in Paul's letter to the Christians in Rome, he does, in fact, call Jesus the Messiah–the Christ.

N. T. Wright, Westminster Abbey
Because the word Christ is a title, not a proper name, we know that

this means that from the very beginning they regarded Jesus as the Messiah. They were interpreting His death in terms of biblical prophecy.

Narrator
Did Jesus of Nazareth truly fulfill all the promises made to Israel about their coming King and Deliverer?

Amy-Jill Levine, Vanderbilt Divinity School
Because I am Jewish, I am often asked, "How come you don't believe in Jesus? He fulfilled all those messianic prophecies you have back in the Old Testament?" There's actually no messianic checklist. It is not as if somebody went through and said, you know, "born in Bethlehem," "Mom has to be a virgin," "Crucified." It's not there.

N. T. Wright, Westminster Abbey
Jesus fulfilled a very great deal of messianic prophecy, yes. But quite a lot of it was fulfilled in ways that people at the time weren't expecting. This is the critical thing.

Paul L. Maier, Professor of Ancient History at Western Michigan University
In Isaiah, chapter 53, we have almost a running commentary on what happened on Good Friday to Jesus.

Narrator
For example, in 750 B.C., the prophet Isaiah wrote these words:

Reader
"He was despised and rejected by men, a man of sorrows, and familiar with suffering. Like one from whom men hide their faces He was despised, and we esteemed Him not . . . But He was pierced for our transgressions, He was crushed for our iniquities; the punishment that brought us peace was upon Him, and by His wounds we are healed . . .We all, like sheep, have gone astray, each of us has turned to his own way; and the LORD has laid on Him the iniquity of us all" [Isaiah 53].

Narrator
And there are others.

Sam Lamerson, Knox Theological Seminary
In Psalm 22 we have a very clear description of the crucifixion. And then, virtually all scholars, probably over 99 percent of New Testament scholars, will agree that Jesus was crucified.

Narrator
For example, King David wrote Psalm 22 in 1000 B.C.

Transcript

Reader
"Dogs have surrounded me; a band of evil men has encircled me, they have pierced my hands and my feet . . . people stare and gloat over me. . . . They divide my garments among them and cast lots for my clothing."

Sam Lamerson, Knox Theological Seminary
Then we ask ourselves, "How is it that this Psalm 22, which clearly describes the Crucifixion and was seen by many, many Jews as a messianic Psalm, happens to fit the fact that Jesus Himself was crucified?" And we say, "Well, it fits that because that's part of God's redemptive history."

Narrator
Traditional scholars believe that in the last 24 hours of Jesus' earthly life, 29 prophecies from the Old Testament were fulfilled. Some of these include: His betrayal by a close friend . . . for 30 pieces of silver . . . His followers would abandon Him . . . He would be accused by false witnesses . . . and would stand silent before them; and, His hands and feet would be pierced.

Paul L. Maier, Professor of Ancient History at Western Michigan University
I think it would be mathematically impossible for anyone else ever to fulfill all these parameters of prophecy in the Old Testament any better than Jesus did.

Narrator
Father Francis Martin on the prophecies Christ fulfilled:

Francis Martin, John Paul II Institute
Suppose you were to find a manuscript, music manuscript, and it contained harmonies—obviously, harmonies to something—and there were brilliant and beautiful passages in there, but the whole thing didn't make sense. Then came the melodic line, and now the whole thing makes sense . . . Jesus is the melodic line to the whole of the Old Testament.

INTRODUCTION TO "RESURRECTION PART 1" SECTION

Dean Jones
Now, Dr. Kennedy, a lot of prophecies relate to Jesus' death. Did his followers expect His crucifixion?

WHO IS THIS JESUS: IS HE RISEN?

D. James Kennedy
No, not at all, Dean. What they expected was that the Messiah was going to overthrow the power of Rome. But what really is unprecedented is what happened after the crucifixion.

Title Graphic: Easter: Fact or Fiction?

Person on the Street
I don't feel silly saying that I believe miracles happen every day.

Person on the Street
Yes, I believe He rose again from the dead, yes.

Person on the Street
As a scientist, I do not believe that Jesus Christ rose from the dead.

Person on the Street
Given yes or no, I would say Jesus Christ rose from the dead.

RESURRECTION

Narrator
The Gospels give us vivid descriptions of Christ's suffering and death.

Catherine Clark Kroeger, Gordon-Conwell Seminary
He is teased and mocked, they hit Him; they strip off His clothes. They put on the pretend raiment of a king. Every shred of dignity was taken from Him.

Narrator
He was nailed to a wooden cross . . . and hung there . . . until dead. Crucified. Why?

Paul L. Maier, Professor of Ancient History at Western Michigan University
According to Christian theology, there was a cosmic dimension to all this. This was more than a man, this was the Son of God, as the centurion claimed at the cross, and that this was part of God's plan of salvation, that Jesus, in fact, should die for our sins.

Narrator
The Gospels tell us He was buried before sundown, just before the Jewish Sabbath began. The body was taken to a tomb, and the massive stone door was rolled closed. Pontius Pilate, the Roman Governor, had already sentenced Christ to death and now wanted to insure the political situation did not get out of hand.

Catherine Clark Kroeger, Gordon-Conwell Seminary

Transcript

Pilate dispatches a contingent of soldiers, probably 15 of them, on each watch.

Narrator
Dr. Catherine Clark Kroeger, Gordon-Conwell Theological Seminary

Catherine Clark Kroeger, Gordon-Conwell Seminary
On top of that, we read that the governor gave his seal. To break that seal on the tomb was to invite death.

Narrator
Crucified and buried on Friday—something extraordinary happened on Sunday morning.

Catherine Clark Kroeger, Gordon-Conwell Seminary
Mary Magdalene comes, and she sees Jesus; she is confronted with the risen Christ.

Narrator
The claim? Jesus rose from the dead—bodily—and appeared to over 500 eyewitnesses in the following 40 days. This is what is reported in the New Testament.

Edwin Yamauchi, Professor of Ancient History at Miami University, Ohio
Christianity, of course, is based on the belief in the resurrection of Jesus. Now, how can you explain the expansion of this religion that exalted a man who suffered the ignominious death, the worst possible death reserved for criminals and slaves, crucifixion? How can you explain the growth and the expansion of this religion without the Resurrection? You cannot. Some scholars have tried to do that, but they do not offer any convincing explanation.

Narrator
Over the course of history, critics have suggested alternative explanations regarding the Resurrection. One view is called the Fraud Theory—that the disciples committed some sort of scam. They either stole the body, they were lying, or some combination of both. Even critics of the Resurrection don't give this theory much weight.

Amy-Jill Levine, Vanderbilt Divinity School
I do not doubt the honesty of those early followers of Jesus. I don't think Jesus' followers made up the Resurrection in order to market something that they had a good take on.

Josh McDowell, Author of *Evidence That Demands A Verdict*
To believe the Fraud Theory, you would have to say that here was a

small band of men—most of them fisherman, just common people—and they came out, fought off the Roman guard, some of the most disciplined soldiers in history, broke the Roman seal that anyone feared breaking because of the consequences, and stole the body. Then they spread abroad that Jesus had been raised from the dead.

Narrator
Another theory, not very popular today, is that Jesus didn't really die; He had passed out, swooned. This view raises as many questions as it answers. The heart of this argument is that after the extreme medical trauma He received in the flogging and on the Cross, He was revived by the cold temperature in the tomb. Dr. Gary Habermas:

Gary Habermas, Author of The Historical Jesus
The Swoon Theory is held by virtually no reputable scholars today. I think there are a number of problems with the Swoon Theory, such as death by crucifixion is essentially death by asphyxiation. You don't get down off the cross alive.

Narrator
This theory would seem to fly in the face of what we know about Rome and their ability to successfully execute prisoners.

Gary Habermas, Author of The Historical Jesus
Second, the nature of the spear wound is that the spear entered the chest cavity and went through the heart. In short, it would have killed Him if He were not already dead.

Josh McDowell, Author of Evidence That Demands A Verdict
Four professional executioners signed His death warrant; that was according to Roman customs. Then, to try to believe that that damp tomb, instead of killing Him, healed Him, and I guess, then He jumped up, hobbled over, pushed the stone out of the way, tied the guard unit up with His linen cloth and appeared to His disciples as the Lord of Life.

Narrator
Another idea is that the disciples were hallucinating when they saw Him raised from the dead. Generally, no two people share the same hallucination, much less 500.

Gary Habermas, Author of The Historical Jesus
The chief problem is the psychological data relating to hallucinations. Hallucinations are not contagious; you can't share them. As a result, virtually no critics hold this theory today at all.

D. A. Carson, Trinity Evangelical Divinity School
It wasn't something they made up. It wasn't something they suddenly

were tricked into. It wasn't one single hallucination. It was event after event after event in which Jesus could be touched and handled, in which He ate with them, in which He talked with them in different settings—different times of day, different light, day and night, over a period of 40 days.

Narrator
Another theory is called the Wrong Tomb Theory—that somehow everyone involved failed to locate the correct burial chamber of Jesus.

Gary Habermas, Author of *The Historical Jesus*
Of course this gets ridiculous. Jesus was laid in the wrong tomb, the guard stood in front of the wrong tomb, the women ran to the wrong tomb, the disciples ran to the wrong tomb, they found the grave cloths in the wrong tomb, nobody knew where the right tomb was, and to touch everything off, Jesus appeared later anyway.

Narrator
Perhaps the most common objection to the bodily resurrection among critical scholars today is the idea that Jesus rose from the dead spiritually, not bodily.

John Dominic Crossan, Former Co-Chairman, The Jesus Seminar
It is absolutely correct to say that the disciples of Jesus, and I myself today, believe in the bodily resurrection of Jesus. But, it has nothing whatsoever to do with a body coming out of the tomb.

Narrator
The idea here is that He was seen by the disciples in visions or epiphanies.

Helmut Koester, Harvard Divinity School
You cannot explain the beginnings of the Christian community without the epiphanies in which Jesus appeared, which confirmed to His disciples and His friends and many others that He was alive after his death. These epiphanies are not, in the first place, evidence for the fact that Jesus is alive.

Narrator
The first problem of this theory is that it simply ignores the claims about the Resurrection that we find in the Gospels.

Edwin Yamauchi, Professor of Ancient History at Miami University, Ohio
The Gospels report that Jesus appeared to them in visible, tangible form. They were able to touch Him; they were able to see Him, and this convinced them that Jesus was, indeed, "risen."

Narrator
The second problem: It fails to consider the revolutionary nature of the claim itself.

Josh McDowell, Author of *Evidence That Demands A Verdict*
If it had been just a spiritual resurrection, the enemies of the New Testament Church would have taken the body of Christ, put it in a cart and walked it right down through the city of Jerusalem and killed Christianity, not in the cradle, but in the womb. There would have been no New Testament Church if they had the body.

Narrator
Summing up, the whole concept of spiritual resurrection is a Greek philosophical idea. The disciples were Jewish. To state that they were proclaiming the Resurrection as only spiritual goes against what we know to be true about the culture and society of the time. Again, while she does not support the traditional Christian concept of the Resurrection, Dr. Levine feels the argument stands on shaky historical ground.

Amy-Jill Levine, Vanderbilt Divinity School
We must remember that Jesus' earliest followers are first century Jews thinking first century Jewish thoughts. Now, if I am one of Jesus' followers, as a first century Jew, and I am convinced that Jesus is the Messiah, I will proclaim that Jesus came back from the dead—not spiritually but physically—because that is what the dominant Jewish thought was at the time.

N. T. Wright, Westminster Abbey
Clearly, for the first century Jews, the word resurrection means the body being reanimated in some way or another. So it's clear that they all did believe that.

Narrator
Underlying all these theories is the premise that no matter what happened after Jesus' death, the bodily resurrection couldn't have occurred.

Jerome Neyrey, University of Notre Dame
One hears this day that miracles are very suspect. The problem is, I think, there is a certain bias against anything supernatural or miraculous in the present day world.

Narrator
The critics assert that science proves such miracles impossible. Dr. Levine reflects this view in explaining why she doesn't believe in the resurrection of Christ.

Transcript

Amy-Jill Levine, Vanderbilt Divinity School
I don't think Jesus' body actually rose from the dead in a physical sense. That so strains my sense of what is possible.

Narrator
Nonetheless, there are thousands of qualified scientists alive today who believe in Jesus Christ's resurrection, such as Dr. Donald Yeomans, astronomer with the Jet Propulsion Lab of NASA.

Donald K. Yeomans, NASA Jet Propulsion Lab
I think it's very possible to be a scientist and believe in Christ as the Messiah. Science routinely deals with things they can't explain, so we can't rule out miracles.

Narrator
Or astronomer Dr. Owen Gingerich of the Harvard-Smithsonian Center for Astro-Physics, who points out that science can't explain what happened that first Easter.

Owen Gingerich, Harvard-Smithsonian Center for Astro-Physics
The resurrection of Jesus is one of those mysteries that is just impossible for us to understand in modern scientific terms.

Narrator
That is because science, by definition, is the study of nature. A miracle, by definition, is supernatural or beyond nature. To argue that you could defend or attack one with the other is a philosophical and logical fallacy.

Josh McDowell, Author of *Evidence That Demands A Verdict*
I think when you look at the overall horizon of the arguments about the Resurrection, I put it this way: the shallowness of the critics speaks louder then the voice of the believer. The lack of refutation. Every year a new theory comes up. Why? Because nothing held water. They are just grasping for something—constantly new theories, new theories, new theories. Why? Because they can't come up with anything solid that refutes it.

INTRODUCTION TO "RESURRECTION, PART 2"

Dean Jones
Now, Dr. Kennedy, is there anything else that backs up that Jesus walked out of that tomb on that first Easter morning?

D. James Kennedy
Indeed there is, Dean. The Grand Canyon wasn't created by a Navaho

WHO IS THIS JESUS: IS HE RISEN?

dragging a stick and the Christian Church, this vast organization, was not created by a myth.

Dean Jones
So what was it created by?

D. James Kennedy
It was created by fact—the fact that Christ was dead, the fact that He rose again from the dead, the disciples saw Him, they talked to Him, they handled Him and they came to believe it was true: He arose from the dead.

Title Graphic: Back From the Dead?

Person On The Street
I believe He rose from the dead.

Person On The Street
I don't believe He rose from the dead.

Person On The Street
He died, He rose, and He did all of this for us.

Person On The Street
No, I do not believe that Jesus rose from the dead.

Person On The Street
I do believe in the Resurrection, but I think it was more of a symbolic thing.

Person On The Street
I do believe that Jesus rose from the dead.

Person On The Street
Well, if I don't believe in that, then why even practice your faith?

Narrator
Now we come to the cornerstone belief of the Christian Church, the idea that Jesus did, indeed, rise from the dead.

N. T. Wright, Westminster Abbey
Often, I think I believe in the resurrection of Jesus like I believe that the sun is shining. Not that I can look directly at it, because you can't, but because in the light of it, I can see everything else.

Bruce Metzger, Princeton Theological Seminary
Certainly, I believe that Jesus Christ rose from the dead.

Francis Martin, John Paul II Institute

Transcript

When we want to say in Hebrew that Christ is risen, we say *hmasiah qum*, that Jesus the Messiah is standing upright. How else do you say it? That is what "resurrection" means.

Catherine Clark Kroeger, Gordon-Conwell Seminary
There are a number of evidences for the resurrection of Jesus.

Narrator
There is, in fact, a great deal of evidence. There are the eyewitness claims we find in the Gospels themselves.

Gary Habermas, Author of *The Historical Jesus*
The earliest eyewitnesses, those who walked and talked with Jesus, are the ones who witnessed His resurrection appearances. Now, the critic is going to have to deal with those claims.

Narrator
This eyewitness reporting is verified by the hostile responses the disciples faced on a daily basis.

Josh McDowell, Author of *Evidence That Demands A Verdict*
There were people, not only believers, but non-believers. I mean there were Gentiles, there were Jews, there was Romans, and many other people who did not agree with the apostles, and they would do anything they could to silence it.

Narrator
Also, there are the already mentioned 500 eyewitnesses.

D. A. Carson, Trinity Evangelical Divinity School
There is no parallel in the ancient world, for example, that has the disclosure of a person risen from the dead to 500 people. There is just nothing like that in the ancient world.

Josh McDowell, Author of *Evidence That Demands A Verdict*
Well, you take 500 people who personally saw Jesus as an eyewitness after the Resurrection, give each one of them six minutes in a court of law to testify, you would have 3,000 minutes of eyewitness testimony; that is 50 hours . . . when in many criminal cases, you only need one eyewitness to convict a person.

Narrator
Another line of reasoning involves the empty tomb.

Paul L. Maier, Professor of Ancient History at Western Michigan University
We often overlook the empty tomb, but I think the empty tomb is very important, because that is something an ancient historian can get at.

WHO IS THIS JESUS: IS HE RISEN?

Narrator
In his book, In The Fullness of Time, Dr. Maier cites Jewish sources dating back to the first century confirming that the tomb was empty.[33]

Paul L. Maier, Professor of Ancient History at Western Michigan University
The evidence is overpowering that the tomb was empty.

Josh McDowell, Author of Evidence That Demands A Verdict
It was the private tomb of Joseph of Arimathea. He was a member of the Sanhedrin. Anyone could locate his tomb. The soldiers were there. Others were there, watching the body of Christ being prepared and buried.

Gary Habermas, Author of The Historical Jesus
The same Jesus who was buried is the Jesus who was raised. For a Jew, that means that the tomb was empty.

Narrator
Another important point: the disciples were not immediately convinced.

Catherine Clark Kroeger, Gordon-Conwell Seminary
The disciples, themselves, were extremely skeptical at first.

Edwin Yamauchi, Professor of Ancient History at Miami University, Ohio
Peter, we know, was discouraged and wanted to quit, but he then was faced with the appearance of Jesus and became the leader of the Church.

Gary Habermas, Author of The Historical Jesus
They weren't just transformed in general. History is full of people who were transformed for all kinds of religious beliefs. I'm saying the disciples were transformed specifically because the Jesus they proclaimed was raised from the dead.

Sam Lamerson, Knox Theological Seminary
Something happened to the disciples to make them at one point afraid, running away, saying, "Our Master has been crucified," to being ready to die for this Jesus. Something happened and the question is "What?" The only thing that really fits the criteria is the Resurrection.

Narrator
These men moved from fear to belief—belief tested in the most severe way imaginable.

Paul L. Maier, Professor of Ancient History at Western Michigan University
Myths do not make martyrs, and if this story had been invented, they

would not have gone to death for it. If Peter had invented the account, as he is ready to be hoisted up on a cross in Rome, he would have blown the whistle and said, "Hold it. I'll plea bargain with you. I will tell you how we did it if I can come off with my life."

Narrator
Of the eleven remaining apostles, the original twelve minus Judas, ten were martyred for their refusal to deny their faith in Jesus Christ. Many were crucified, some stabbed to death, others beheaded.

Sam Lamerson, Knox Theological Seminary
Those people who died did so knowing that it was going to be painful, knowing that it was going to be embarrassing, knowing that it was going to be terror-filled. Yet, they did it anyway as a direct result of the fact that they believed that Jesus Christ was God. They lived in the first century; we live in the twenty-first century, and it seems to me that it is the height of arrogance for us to say in the twenty-first century, "You, all you people who died, you were just foolish; you just didn't know any better. And, we, now . . . we scholars, we know a lot better then you do."

Narrator
Additional evidence for the extraordinary change in the disciples is found in first century history.

N. T. Wright, Westminster Abbey
The interesting thing about the early Christians is not just that they were transformed from being a dejected and a despairing, frightened little group into being a dynamic, lively, and outgoing and brave group, though that's true too, but it is that they didn't get another Messiah. They said Jesus was the Messiah.

Richard A. Horsley, University of Massachusetts, Boston
One of the things I've spent a good bit of time on myself is with the movements that seem parallel to Jesus and His movement. There were prophets, one of them named Theudas and another one who was an Egyptian Jewish prophet, who led their followers out into the wilderness, expecting that God was going to carry out some new act of liberation, give the people freedom back in their own land. Now, of course, the Roman authorities immediately sent out the troops and brought their heads back on a pole and their followers, as far as we know, simply dispersed.

N. T. Wright, Westminster Abbey
The disciples, at the time of Jesus' crucifixion, were completely devastated. Everybody in their world knew that if you were following a prophet or a messiah or a leader or whatever and that person got ex-

ecuted by the Roman authorities, it meant you had backed the wrong horse. Since everybody knew that a crucified Messiah was a failed Messiah, the only thing that explains why they said Jesus was the Messiah is that they really did believe He had been bodily raised from the dead.

Narrator
Finally, many scholars argue that the amazing growth of the Church itself is evidence of a resurrected Christ.

Sam Lamerson, Knox Theological Seminary
I think the best piece of evidence for the Resurrection of Christ is the fact that the Church exists today. There were lots of messiahs that existed in the first century, many of whom were killed by the Roman government. But there's only one Christian Church.

Paul L. Maier, Professor of Ancient History at Western Michigan University
Where did Christianity first begin in terms of the organized proclamation that Jesus rose from the dead? Only one place on earth: Jerusalem. There, least of all, could Christianity ever have gotten started if the moldering body of Jesus of Nazareth were available anytime after Sunday morning.

N. T. Wright, Westminster Abbey
What we're looking at with the Resurrection is the birth of God's new world, of a whole new mode of being. That is why I think the disciples found it so incredibly difficult to get their minds turned around right from the beginning. They were absolutely clear that the tomb was empty, that they had seen Jesus, and that this really was that which the prophets had spoken about, even though they weren't expecting it. So, I believe it, because, as a Christian, all my life I have found that it makes sense of everything else. But, as a historian, I find that all the lines point in towards saying, "This is far and away the best explanation for why early Christianity began and why it told the stories it did."

CONCLUDING CONVERSATION

Dean Jones
Well, now, if people truly believed that Jesus walked out of that Judean tomb on that first Easter morning, wouldn't it settle a lot of arguments?

D. James Kennedy
Indeed, it would. The fact is that millions and millions of people

have become convinced that He did walk out of that tomb and that the evidence compellingly points to the fact of the Resurrection. That's why the Christian Church today is the largest institution that does or has ever existed on this planet.

Dean Jones
And the evidence that we've seen today has pointed in that direction.

D. James Kennedy
That's right, Dean, He was dead, but He walked out of the tomb, and the world has never been the same.

Dean Jones
Dr. Kennedy, we've spent an hour answering the question: Who is this Jesus? Now would you sum it up and would you personalize it for us? What does He mean to you?

D. James Kennedy
Well, Dean, I was in my mid-20s when I was first confronted by this person, Jesus, and who He was and what He came to do. I discovered that He came to die for me, to pay for my transgressions, and wonder of wonders, to offer me eternal life, freely, as a gift. I was astonished. I invited Him into my life, and Dean, everything was changed. I became a new person in Christ.

Dean Jones
And it all goes back to what the Bible says?

D. James Kennedy
Yes. And I discovered that Jesus is not only human, but He is divine.

Dean Jones
Thank you, Dr. Kennedy. Ladies and gentlemen, thank you for joining us, we hope you have enjoyed this special presentation and that you're closer to understanding. . . . who is this Jesus?

D. James Kennedy
How about you, my dear friend? Has Christ transformed your life? I would urge you to invite Him to come into your life and forgive you, and cleanse you, and change you today. Would you like to do that? If so, pray with me, right now, this prayer of commitment: Lord Jesus Christ, I believe that you died for me and paid for all of my transgressions. Cleanse me. Forgive me. I place my trust in you. I repent of my sins. From this day forward I desire to follow You and to live for You. Use my life for your glory. I pray it in your holy name, Amen."[34]

Soli Deo Gloria.

ENDNOTES

1. Winner of a 2001 Angel Award and of an award from the International NY Film & TV Festival 2001.
2. This chapter is largely based on Chapter 2 of D. James Kennedy and Jerry Newcombe, *The Gates of Hell Shall Not Prevail* (Nashville: Thomas Nelson, Publishers, 1996).
3. Josh McDowell, *Evidence That Demands a Verdict* (San Bernadino, Calif.: Campus Crusade for Christ, 1972), 209.
4. Quoted in ibid., 214.
5. Ibid., 223.
6. Ibid.
7. Transcript from a TV interview with Jerry Newcombe, Ft. Lauderdale, Fla., Spring 1988.
8. McDowell, 179.
9. Hills Lectures in Divinity, Vol. I, pp. 47, 48. Quoted in William Taylor, *The Miracles of Our Saviour* (New York: Hodder and Stoughton, 1890), 21 22.
10. McDowell, 233.
11. Ibid., 244.
12. Ibid., 248 255.
13. One of the reasons he came to believe this was because it says in John 5:2, "Now there *is* in Jerusalem by the Sheep Gate a pool . . . " [emphasis mine] When the Roman Titus came in 70 A.D., he thoroughly destroyed Jerusalem and much of Israel. So Robinson believed, therefore, that John, the final Gospel, was written before 70 A.D.
14. Gary Habermas, *The Historical Jesus: Ancient Evidence for the Life of Christ* (Joplin, Missouri, College Press Publishing Company, 1996), 187-228.
15. See Pierre Barbet, *A Doctor At Calvary: The Passion of Our Lord Jesus Christ as Described by a Surgeon*, trans. by the Earl of Wicklow (New York: P.J. Kenedy & Sons, 1953).
16. Quoted in John C. Iannone, "Credibly Discrediting the Carbon-14 Test on the Shroud," in *The Mystery of the Shroud of Turin* (Staten Island, NY: Alba House, 1998), 168.
17. Ibid., 169.

Transcript

18 Mary and Alan Whanger, *The Shroud of Turin: An Adventure of Discovery* (Franklin, Tenn.: Providence House Publishers, 1998), 105, 107.

19 Marc Antonacci, *The Resurrection of the Shroud: New Scientific, Medical and Archaeological Evidence* (New York: M. Evans and Company, Inc., 2000), 157.

20 David Van Biema, "Science and the Shroud," *Time*, 20 April, 1998, 61.

21 Ibid.

22 Ian Wilson, *The Turin Shroud* (Middlesex, England: Penguin Books, 1978).

23 Antonacci, 8-9.

24 Van Biema, 57.

25 D. James Kennedy and Jerry Newcombe, *What If Jesus Had Never Been Born?* (Nashville: Thomas Nelson, Publishers, 1994), 178.

26 Request your free copy of *Beginning Again* today. Write to D. James Kennedy Ministries, P.O. Box 7009, Albert Lea, MN 56007 or call 1-800-988-7884.

27 Written and produced by Jerry Newcombe, Steve Zeoli, and Gary Fallon with additional input from Donald T. Robinson III and Susan Dzuro.

28 The Ancient Spanish Monastery in North Miami Beach, Florida, is the oldest building in the Western Hemisphere. It was first built in Spain in 1141 and fell into disuse in the 1800s. William Randolph Hearst purchased it in 1925 to use it to surround a swimming pool, but he died before it was ever reassembled in the United States in the early 1950s. Today it is an Episcopalian church, St. Bernard of Clairvaux. It is listed in the National Registry of Historical Places.

29 Matthew 24; Mark 13; Luke 21.

30 Here's just one example of such evidence: Mark is widely believed to have been written before Matthew and before Luke. Luke's Gospel is quoted as "Scripture" in 1 Timothy 5:18, which was written in A.D. 62 or 63. That would make both Mark and Luke written prior to A.D. 62 or 63.

31 Let's delve further into the Jesus Seminar. The critical point to understand is that there was no new evidence in the Scripture that drove them to their conclusions; it was rather their own liberal approach that led them even to undertake the project in the first place. The Jesus Seminar is best understood as worn out, liberal theologians who have turned to a publicist instead of the truth—the Jesus of Scripture. The late Dr. James Montgomery Boice of Tenth Presbyterian Church in Philadelphia pointed out the Jesus Seminar is "really an example of liberal ministers and professors coming out of the closet. All they're really doing is in *public* what they do in a more private way in the classroom and in their own studies." Dr. Boice stated the obvious: "Imagine a group of scholars, now, two thousand years from the time that Jesus lived and whose words were written down by eye witnesses, a group of scholars *two*

thousand years later voting in a meeting on what Jesus really said and what He didn't. That is laughable."

"It just seems like the more preposterous you can be," observes theologian and best-selling author R. C. Sproul, "the more radical you can be, the easier it is to get a degree or to get a hearing in certain academic circles."

"Liberal" and "unbelieving" are synonymous when it comes to theology. So the Jesus Seminar is essentially unbelieving scholars sharing their unbelief. When they ask a question like, "Did Jesus make this statement or not?" and then vote on that anonymously, as the Jesus Seminar did, what they're voting on is simply their own prejudices. There is nothing in the historic record, nothing in the Biblical manuscripts, that supports what they say. And while manuscripts may differ in places when it comes to spelling or words, they are in complete agreement in *every* point of theology.

So, if there are any things in question, they are all listed in the critical apparatus of the Greek New Testament. But the people of the Jesus Seminar were not dealing with the *manuscript* evidence, they were dealing with, frankly, their own opinions, and with extra biblical writings (primarily, the 2nd century document, the Gospel of Thomas—which the early Church decidedly rejected as Gnostic heresy).

The sections in the gospels where manuscripts do differ in spelling or in words include only 1 or 2 percent of the text, if that. The New Testament documents are very reliable. What the Jesus Seminar has done is to get rid of 82 percent of the text. Textually, they stand on quicksand.

An important book rebutting the Jesus Seminar from an evangelical perspective is *Jesus Under Fire: Modern Scholarship Reinvents the Historical Jesus*, edited by Michael J. Wilkins and J. P. Moreland. Among those who have written essays for this book is Dr. Gary Habermas, author and co-author of numerous books on the historicity of Jesus Christ. In the chapter entitled "Where Do We Start Studying Jesus?" on pages 43-44, Denver Seminary professor Craig Blomberg has this to say about the group:

> The Jesus Seminar and its friends do not reflect any consensus of scholars except for those on the "radical fringe" of the field. Its methodology is seriously flawed and its conclusions unnecessarily skeptical.... The conservative nature of oral tradition in ancient Judaism, particularly among disciples who revered their rabbi's words, makes it highly likely that Jesus' teaching would have been carefully preserved, even given a certain flexibility in the specific wording with which it was reported ... there is a huge volume of scholarship to support the picture of Christ that Matthew, Mark, Luke, and John portray.

32 Part of the Holyland Experience, Orlando, Florida.

33 See Paul L. Maier, *In the Fulness of Time: A Historian Looks at Christmas, Easter, and the Early Church* (Grand Rapids: Kregel Publications, 1991), 197-205.

34 Again, I encourage you to write for your free copy of *Beginning Again*. Write

to D. James Kennedy Ministries, P.O. Box 7009, Albert Lea, MN 56007 or call 1-800-988-7884. God bless you.

INDEX

Abgar V, King, 32
Adler, Alan, 30
Antonacci, Marc, 27, 38, 93
Augustus, 63, 75

Barbet, Pierre, 24, 92
Bar-Serapion, Mara, 16
Boston College, 60
Buddha, Buddhism, 5, 44
Byzantine Empire, 33

Caesar, Julius, 70, 75
Caiaphas, 76
Carbon-dating of the Shroud of Turin, 26-28, 34, 92
Carlyle, Thomas, 41
Carson, D. A., 51-52, 54-56, 67, 69, 82, 87
Christian Science, 10, 11
Columbine, 43
Crossan, John Dominic, 49, 51-52, 60, 65-67, 72, 74, 83
Crown of Thorns, 23, 30

Da Vinci, Leonardo, 36
David, King, 78
Dead Sea Scrolls, 69
deCharny, Geoffrey, 21
DeLeon, Ponce, 41
DeVos, Helen, 49
DeVos, Richard, 49
Disciples (transformation of after Christ's resurrection), 4, 11-13, 15, 89

Eliot, T. S., 41
Empty Tomb, 6, 87

Filas, Fr. Francis, 25
Fixx, Jim, 41

500 people (Christ's resurrected appearance to), 7, 11, 14, 81-82, 87
Flagrum, Roman, 22
Fraud Theory, 8-10, 81
Funk, Robert, 35, 66

Gingerich, Owen, 85
Grand Canyon, 5, 85

Habermas, Gary, 16, 52, 72, 82-83, 87-88, 92, 94
Hadrian, 16
Hallucination Theory, 13
Harvard, 14, 51
Harvard Divinity School, 50,-51, 55-57, 66, 77, 83
Harvard-Smithsonian Center for
    Astro-Physics, 85
Harvey, Paul, 39
Hill, Principal, 9
Hinduism, 44
Homer, 70
Horsley, Richard A., 50, 52, 59, 65, 74, 89

Islam (see also Mohammed, Muslims), 44

Jainism, 44
Jehovah's Witnesses, 12
Jennings, Peter, 2
Jesus Seminar, 35, 49, 51,-52, 60, 64-67, 72, 74, 83, 93, 94
John, Apostle, 7, 15-16, 45-46, 53-54, 56, 60, 68, 75, 92, 94
John Paul II Institute, 49-50, 61, 63, 65, 79, 86
Johnson, Samuel, 40
Jones, Dean, 2, 49-53, 58, 63-64, 67-68, 71, 73, 76, 79, 85-86, 90-91
Joseph of Arimathea, 15, 20, 88
Josephus, 16, 71-72
Julius Caesar, 70

Knox Theological Seminary, 1, 51-52, 62, 70, 75, 78-79, 88-90
Koester, Helmut, 50-51, 55-57, 66, 77, 83
Koran, 13, 71
Kreeft, Peter, 64
Kroeger, Catherine Clark, 51, 80-81, 87-88

Lake, Kirsopp, 14
Lamerson, Sam, 51, 62, 70, 75, 78-79, 88-90
Lamont, Corliss, 42
Lao-tse, 5, 44
Legend Theory, 15

Index

Levine, Amy-Jill, 52, 54, 66, 69, 78, 81, 84-85
Lewis, C. S., 60
Lucian, 16

Maier, Paul L., 49, 52, 57, 62-63, 67-69, 72-75, 78-80, 87-90, 94
Mandylion, 33
Marino, Fr. Joseph, 26
Martin, Fr. Francis, 49-50, 61, 63, 65, 79, 86
Mary (Mother of Jesus), 13, 62, 75
Mary Magdalene, 81
Massey, James D., 49
Massey, Millicent, 49
McDowell, Josh, 7-8, 49, 60-61, 81-82, 84-85, 87-88, 92
Meacham, William, 26
Messianic Prophecies, 77
Miami University, Ohio, 73, 76, 81, 83, 88
Miracles, 10, 16-17, 56-58, 60-61, 65, 80, 84-85
Mohammed, 5, 13
Muslims, 13, 32, 33

NASA, 29, 36, 85
Nero, 7
Neyrey, Jerome, 66, 84
Notre Dame, 51, 66, 84

Paul, Apostle, 18, 54, 77
Peter, Apostle, 15, 16, 54, 88-89
Phlegon, 16, 73
Pia, Secundo, 29
Pilate, Pntius, 13, 25, 72, 75, 80, 81
Plato, 70
Pliny the Younger, 16, 73
Princeton Theological Seminary, 51, 55-56, 70, 73

Samworth, Herbert, 69
Sanhedrin, 7, 13-16, 88
Shakespeare, William, 43, 44
Shroud of Turin Research Project
    (STURP), 21, 26, 30
Spiritual Resurrection Theory, 12
Sproul, R. C., 52, 94
Strauss, David Friedrich, 11
STURP (See Shroud of Turin Research Project)
Sudarium of Oveida, 25
Suetonius, 16, 73

97

Swoon Theory, 10, 11, 30, 82

Tacitus, 16, 72
Talmud, 16
Thallus, 16, 73
Trajan, 16, 73
Trinity Evagelical Divinity School, 51, 54-56, 67, 69, 82, 87

University of Massachusetts, Boston, 50, 52, 59, 65, 74, 89

Vanderbilt Divinity School, 52, 54, 66, 69, 78, 81, 84-85
Via Dolorosa, 75
VP8-Image Analyzer, 29, 36

Western Michigan university, 49, 52, 57, 62-63, 67-69, 72-75, 78-80, 87-88, 90
Westminster Abbey, 51-52, 59, 70-71, 76-78, 84, 86, 89-90
Whanger, Alan, 23, 27, 35, 37, 93
Whanger, Mary, 93
Wilson, Ian, 32, 38, 93
Wright, N. T., 51-52, 59, 70-71, 76-78, 84, 86, 89-90
Wrong Tomb Theory, 14, 83

Yamauchi, Edwin, 73, 76, 81, 83, 88
Yarbrough, Robert, 56
Yeomans, Donald K., 85

Zoroastrianism, 44

About the Authors

DR. D. JAMES KENNEDY (1930-2007) was the most listened-to Presbyterian minister in history because of his internationally syndicated television and radio broadcasts. For 48 years, he was the senior pastor of Coral Ridge Presbyterian Church in Fort Lauderdale, Florida, where Evangelism Explosion International was launched. Kennedy authored 70 books, including the bestsellers, *Evangelism Explosion*, *Why I Believe*, and (with Dr. Jerry Newcombe) *What If Jesus Had Never Been Born?* He founded Coral Ridge Ministries (now known as D. James Kennedy Ministries), Westminster Academy, and Knox Theological Seminary. In 2005, he was inducted into the National Religious Broadcasters' "Hall of Fame."

DR. JERRY NEWCOMBE serves as the co-host of *Kennedy Classics* and as spokesman for D. James Kennedy Ministries. He has produced or co-produced more than 60 one-hour national television specials for D. James Kennedy Ministries (formerly Coral Ridge Ministries) and is the author or co-author of 24 books, including two bestsellers, *What If Jesus Had Never Been Born* (with Dr. D. James Kennedy) and *George Washington's Sacred Fire* (with Dr. Peter Lillback). Jerry has also been a guest on numerous talk shows including *Janet Parshall's America*, *Politically Incorrect with Bill Maher*, *Point of View*, and the Fox News Channel, and he writes a weekly opinion column that is hosted by D. James Kennedy Ministries and several online publications.

SPECIAL THANKS

We are most grateful to Dr. Alan and Mary Whanger for their meticulous review of Chapter 2.